Early Childhood Education

History, Philosophy and Experience

Early Childhood Education

History, Philosophy and Experience

Cathy Nutbrown, Peter Clough
and Philip Selbie

Los Angeles • London • New Delhi • Singapore

SAGE Publications Ltd
1 Oliver's Yard
55 City Road
London EC1Y 1SP

SAGE Publications Inc.
2455 Teller Road
Thousand Oaks, California 91320

SAGE Publications India Pvt Ltd
B 1/I 1 Mohan Cooperative Industrial Area
Mathura Road
New Delhi 110 044

SAGE Publications Asia-Pacific Pte Ltd
33 Pekin Street #02-01
Far East Square
Singapore 048763

Library of Congress Control Number: 2007940394

British Library Cataloguing in Publication data

A catalogue record for this book is available from the British Library

ISBN 978-1-4129-4497-7
ISBN 978-1-4129-4498-4 (pbk)

Typeset by C&M Digitals, Pvt Ltd, Chennai, India
Printed By Cromwell Press, Trowbridge, Wiltshire, England
Printed on paper from sustainable resources

For the new pioneers ...

Contents

About the authors

Cathy Nutbrown is Professor of Education at the University of Sheffield where she directs MA and EdD programmes in Early Childhood Education. Before joining the School of Education at Sheffield she worked as a nursery teacher and advisory teacher in Sheffield. Her publications include: *Threads of Thinking* (Sage); *Key Concepts in Early Childhood Education and Care* (Sage); *Early Literacy Work with Families: Policy, Practice and Research* (Sage). Cathy's current research focuses on the Arts in the early years.

Peter Clough is Professor of Inclusive Education at Liverpool Hope University. He has taught in all phases of education and, before moving to Hope, was Professor at Queen's University Belfast. Peter's publications include *Narrative and Fictions in Educational Research* (OUP); *Theories of Inclusive Education* (Sage) and *Inclusion in the Early Years* (Sage). Peter's current research interests centre around artistic portrayal of inclusive research issues.

Philip Selbie is a lecturer in Early Childhood Studies at the University of Plymouth. Previously he taught in reception classes in Southampton and in Prague, Czech Republic and led the early years department in an international school in Prague. Philip's current research interest is in work of in Jan Amos Komensky.

Acknowledgements

We should like to thank the numerous people who have shared their ideas with us and allowed them to try out some of the ideas in this book with them. We are particularly grateful to those who read the conversations and commented on them. Special thanks go to our students who told us how important it was to bring the ideas of past pioneers alive and commented on our attempts to do this. The keepers of the archives we consulted have been particularly helpful. We thank Sheffield LEA for allowing us to quote from their 1987 Nursery Education Guidelines. We wish to acknowledge the important contributions played by Marianne Lagrange, Sophie Cox and Jeanette Graham in the production of his book.

Introduction

With burgeoning development in the field of early childhood education and care, and new interest in alternative approaches to early years provision internationally, there is a danger that an understanding of the histories and legacies on which present-day provision for care and education is built might be allowed to slip away. There is the potential, amidst constant and persistent policy changes, that those whose work involves a concern with early childhood education will have fewer and fewer opportunities to ask where ideas began, how ideas and practices have developed and what roots lie beneath present-day practices and philosophical ideas.

This book traces some historical ideas and their pioneers. It provides brief biographies and critical insights into their work and compares their principles and practices to those of others past and present.

This book takes an innovative and accessible approach to the history and philosophy of early childhood education. It gives necessary, meaningful detail about individual educators and contributors to the field in order to help readers understand how contributions and developments in the past have created routes to present thinking and practice. We then work with their ideas and hold them up to interrogation in the light of twenty-first-century life; test them, to see what such thinkers and practitioners might still have to offer the field of early childhood education and care today.

In this way, the book offers four things:

- A historical overview of the development of some key ideas and practices in early childhood education
- A series of biographical accounts of some 24 key contributors to the field, with summaries of their major achievements and key texts
- An exploration of the ways in which their individual ideas compare with others through imagined conversations based on their writings
- An analysis of ways in which certain common themes can be seen in both earlier writings and current practices, and an exploration of how ideas of past pioneers might be interpreted and incorporated in modern-day early childhood provision.

1 A Short History of Early Childhood Education

The legacy of history

> Without words, without writing and without books there would be no history, there could be no concept of humanity.
> Hermann Hesse (1877–1962), winner of the Nobel Prize for Literature in 1946

We begin this book with a short chronology of developments in thinking and practice which have taken place in the history of early childhood education in the UK. We have identified some key moments and key international figures in history who have, in different ways, influenced thinking, research, policy and practice in the development of education and care for the youngest children. In opening the book with an overview of early years developments from the 1600s to the present day we have created a foundation for the rest of the book, and we have shown our view of the impact of individual men and women who, in one way or another, made their distinctive mark on the development of early childhood education.

History is what humanity creates, and policy itself is *real*ised by people; as Hesse (1939) reminds us, history helps to generate a concept of humanity. In the sense that people *are* the history-makers, early childhood educators *make* both history and policy, though in another sense the inheritance of history is something from which they stand apart and the impact of policy is something over which they may feel they have no control. But, as Merleau-Ponty (1962) has it, 'although we are born into a [pre-existing] world, we [yet] have the task of creating it ...' (p. ix).

One of the aims of this book is to help readers to consider current policies and practices in early childhood education through the lens of history; it seeks to use history as a means of understanding present states and challenges of early childhood education and as a tool for informing the shape of early childhood education in the future – that is, in our *own* lives and careers.

Of course, we could say that nothing is new, and ideas simply recur; perhaps most topical at the end of the twentieth century was the example of the planned re-introduction of 'Payment by Results' signalled in a Department for Education and Employment (DfEE) Green Paper (DfEE 1999) with echoes of 'Payment by Results' in the Revised Code of 1862, where the notion of raising standards through the use of testing was introduced and teachers' pay was linked to the achievement of their pupils. This is not so much a case of history repeating itself but perhaps more an example of how events, developments and ideas can rhyme, or chime, or echo over time.

This book is structured to encourage critical engagement with historical ideas and developments, influences on early childhood education, issues of policy development and implementation, and the impact of research on policy. The development of early childhood education provision, and the key figures in that development, form the starting points for considering where early childhood education has come from and where present policies 'fit', or do not fit, with the lessons of history. The ways in which childhood has been constructed throughout recent history is also a topic which helps to inform the critique of policy which has moved from the central aim of 'nurturing childhood' to a situation where 'raising educational achievement' is the main goal. Central to this argument about the shift in priorities of policy in early childhood education is the change in language and the new terminologies imposed year after year upon early childhood education.

Finally, we are aware that there is no single history; it needs always to be seen from multiple perspectives, viewed through different lenses. In understanding what has happened in the UK, it is important, too, to look at international developments in early childhood education and the many influences from figures throughout history working around the world.

Early childhood education in the UK: a brief history

During the mid 1700s there were moves in political and social spheres to provide some form of education for young children. 'Monitorial' schools were set up from the end of the 1700s by the Quaker, Joseph Lancaster, and the New Lanark worksite elementary school was established by Robert Owen in the early 1800s. The National Society was founded in 16 October 1811; its aim:

... that the National Religion should be made the foundation of National Education, and should be the first and chief thing taught to the poor, according to the excellent Liturgy and Catechism provided by our Church.[1]

The National Society established a national system of education, supplemented by the State from 1870. In 2007 there were some 5,000 Church of England and Church in Wales schools (originally known as National Schools), most of which are primary schools, educating almost a million children. However, it was the protestant 'Evangelicals' who, through the Home and Colonial School Society (founded in 1836), had the insight to consider the development of schools for the youngest children and open 'infant schools'.

Thus, throughout the eighteenth and nineteenth centuries schools were being developed and systems devised and expanded, not only by religious organisations and benefactors, but also of course by the socially and politically motivated who were driven, not by religious conviction but by a belief that the education of young children could contribute to the development of a better society. By 1862, the Revised Code was introduced whereby grants were awarded to elementary schools, depending upon the achievement of their pupils. Forster's Education Act of 1870 established school boards in areas where there was a lack of elementary school provision.

Simultaneously, there was pioneering work on the nature of curriculum for young children, with the Mundella Code of 1882 advocating 'enlightened' teaching of young children. Particular figures can be seen as distinctly influential in such 'curricular development' (though of course it would not have been known as such!); these include: Johann Pestalozzi, Friedrich Froebel, Rachel and Margaret McMillan, Maria Montessori, Charlotte Mason and Susan Isaacs. All advocated ways of working with children which centred around the children themselves and where play was a central component of what was offered.

It was the development of industry which first prompted schooling for young children, and discussion about the age at which compulsory schooling should begin. The view was put forward in parliament during the enactment of Forster's Education Act (1870) that sending children to school a year earlier than some other countries in Europe would give them some sort of advantage in educational achievement (Szretzer 1964). Indeed, it was Mundella who, in an address to the 'National Education League', said: 'I ask you Englishmen and Englishwomen, are Austrian children to be educated before English children?' (National Education League 1869: 133). A further reason, put forward in the Hadow Report of

---

[1] (http://www.natsoc.org.uk/society/history)

1911, for supporting an early start to schooling was the desire to prevent childhood ill-health by the introduction of medical inspections of young children while at school. An early start to compulsory schooling was paralleled by early leaving too, a view supported by the industrialists who needed young workers.

Later, during the First World War years and the need for mothers of younger children to work, the development of nursery education flourished. The following account of the setting up of nursery education in Sheffield is typical of many cities in the North of England.

The Development of Nursery Education in Sheffield has paralleled National trends. Nursery Education began in this country at the beginning of [the twentieth] century at the instigation of people who were concerned about the plight of children in industrial cities: Sheffield children were typical of these. The social climate was such that by the late 1920s Sheffield was beginning to suffer in the Depression: unemployment was rife and poverty was very real. The then centre of the city buildings consisted of many terraced houses and factories, with little opportunity for the children to grow and develop in a healthy environment. In Scotland, Robert Owen had seen the necessity for young children to have good food, fresh air and rest in uncrowded conditions and started a nursery for his workers' children at the turn of the century. Rachel and Margaret McMillan began their Nursery School in Deptford with the intention of providing an 'open-air' school for young children in 1913. This was the beginning of thinking that young children needed special provision.

Children from poorer areas were often under-nourished with poor skin and pale complexions: rickets were common. Colds, coughs and catarrh seemed to perpetuate. Clothing was inadequate and unattractive: there was very little colour in their lives. The children were often stitched into their clothes for winter. Flea bites, sore eyes and lack of sleep were common and infection was easily passed on. The local Women Councillors (in Sheffield) decided to fight for a nursery school and, although it was an uphill battle, Denby Street Nursery School was opened in 1928 based on the McMillan open-shelter type. It was open from 8.30 a.m. to 5.00 p.m. and holidays. There was practically no money, very little equipment and a skeleton staff.

The emphasis was on physical care. The children were fed, washed, rested and loved. The food was simple and plentiful – buttered rusks, dripping toast, hash stew, shepherd's pie, lentil roast, milk puddings, custard and fruit and steamed puddings. The nurse and doctor visited regularly. Cod liver oil was administered and children monitored for impetigo, rickets, poor eyesight, etc. School became a haven especially if children were from families living in only one room, although the schools were very careful not to usurp the home.

Outdoor play was robust and skilful as many of the children had played in the streets from a very young age. The imaginative play – particularly domestic play – was very real. The children were independent, practical, capable and resilient, many having to be so from a very young age, especially if they came from a large family.

Sheffield Nursery Education grew slowly from its beginnings: there were only 4 nursery schools by 1939 when most children were evacuated or spent quite a lot of time in the air raid shelters after the outbreak of war. Nurseries did close at the beginning of the war but opened again in 1940 on a short-time basis because of the bombing campaign. Gradually the day became extended again as it was felt that children could catch up on sleep at the nursery and there was a need for the regular routine and stability it provided.

The war years did give an impetus to nursery education: there was some expansion because of the demand for married women in the labour force. The expansion of nursery education became a high priority and resources were found. For example in 1941 a new joint circular was sent out to set up special war nurseries financed by the Ministry of Health and the Maternity and Child Welfare Department. The full-time nurseries were open in some cases for 12–15 hours and only for children of working mothers. Part-time nurseries also gave priority to evacuated children and those of working mothers. The emphasis moved to include children's social and emotional needs.

Although the extension in provision of nursery education because of the pressures of war was considerable, compared with earlier years, it could not be regarded as 'spectacular' as only a very small proportion of the total child population in the age group were receiving some kind of nursery education. However, the war nurseries did much to popularise the idea of a nursery stage in education. In the emergency situation of the war, where married women were needed to work, the care of the children had been met by the nursery school. The idea that only mothers can look after children, lost its force during the war.

The 1944 Education Act implied that nursery education would become universal but the 50s and 60s marked a decline in state provision for a variety of reasons – economic pressures, demand for space and teachers for the over fives during the 'bulge' years. (Government) Circular 8/60 effectively stopped expansion until Addendum No. 2 in 1965 when a controlled expansion was allowed where this would increase the return to service of married women teachers.

In 1960, however, the Pre-school Playgroup Movement was formed, the lack of nursery places having given mothers the impetus to make their own provision. The continuous expansion of the movement and the commitment and dedication of those working in it has contributed significantly to greater awareness of the needs of the under fives.

Interest in the state provision of nursery education came to the fore once again when stimulated by the Plowden Report in 1967. It was recommended that nursery classes should be extended, and that an immediate start on building of new nursery schools should be made in 'educational priority areas': the idea being that good nursery schools could begin to offset the consequences of social deprivation. (Sheffield LEA 1986: 2–3)

Meanwhile, during the same period, in Scotland, following Robert Owen's initiatives, Nursery Education began with voluntary contributions in the early 1900s through the commitment of those who saw the need to provide something particular for younger children:

At the beginning of the 20th century as people became more aware of social and physical conditions, public interest was directed to the welfare of children under five years old. The first nursery school in Scotland was opened in Edinburgh in 1903.

Edinburgh's Free Kindergarten was established in 1903. Miss Howden, infant headmistress at Milton House School in 1881, who was concerned at 'babies' accompanying siblings to school, left her savings to found the free kindergarten which started in Galloway's Entry, Canongate in 1903.

St Saviour's Child Garden was established in 1906 by Miss Lileen Hardy in co-operation with Canon Laurie, Rector of Old St Pauls Episcopal Church in the church's hall in Browns Close. (Hardy, 1919:7)

Thus, His Majesty's Inspector of Schools (HMI) reported in 1913:

> This school is a bright spot in a rather dark neighbourhood ... with two groups of about 20 children under 5 years of age. To these school lessons are not given. They engage in a variety of interesting kindergarten occupations and they learn to draw and sing. The rest of the time they spend taking care of pets, in attempts at gardening and in playing at housework. They mostly live in the open air and are obviously happy. Regular lessons in elementary subjects are given to those children whose ages are from 5–7 years. (City of Edinburgh Council/Early Education 1999)

All such developments in early education had social and welfare issues at their heart, as fundamental concerns. These, combined with the effects of war years and a recognition of the needs of young children, fuelled the development of early education provision, where establishments set up to care for the physical needs of young children also began to develop ways of providing opportunities for young children to learn. The summary of the HMI report on St Saviour's school describes what many would recognise as elements of an appropriate curriculum for young children. Extended opening hours for working mothers was often normal practice and balancing children's needs was a central feature of many nursery establishments.

Foundation stones: some key figures whose work has influenced thinking and development of provision for young children

The following section outlines some of the politicians, social pioneers, academics, industrialists, and educationalists who in different ways contributed to the development of early education in the UK. Table 1.1 provides a brief summary (in chronological order of date of birth) of some of the figures who influenced these developments in the UK, up to the early 1960s. This summary helps to identify 'key moments' in particular periods of history, and the links between various pioneers and the development of policies. It is not a comprehensive summary, but serves to provide an indicative 'archaeology' behind current UK practices.

Table 1.1   Some influential figures and key events in the development of early education in the UK, up to the early 1960s

Born	Died	Name	Summary of achievements
1592	1670	Jan Amos Komenský (Comenius)	In 1631 published *The School of Infancy* focusing on the early years of a child's education and, in particular, education by mothers within the home. In 1658 his *Orbis Sensualium Pictus*, the first picture book for children, was published.
1712	1778	Jean-Jacques Rousseau	In 1762 published *Emile* which expounded his view for a universal system of education through the experience of the child Emile.
1746	1827	Johann Heinrich Pestalozzi	1780: Published *Leonard and Gertrude: A Book for the People* in which he set out a view of education as central to the regeneration of a community. He wrote: 'The school ought really to stand in closest connection with the life of the home'. He believed that mothers should be educated sufficiently to teach their children at home.
1771	1858	Robert Owen	Mill owner in New Lanark, Scotland. 1816: Established schools for children of his workers. Schools were for children under 12 years with particular emphasis on the infant school. James Buchanan was the first teacher in the New Lanark school, exemplifying Owens' ideals of kindness, activity and co-operation.
1771	1855	Joshua Watson	A retired wine merchant and government contractor during the Napoleonic Wars, he was once referred to by Bishop Lloyd of Oxford as 'the best layman in England', was an influential Church of England figure in the nineteenth century, and one of the founders of the National Society for the Education of the Poor in the Principles of the Established Church in 1811.
1778	1838	Joseph Lancaster	One of the founders of mass education for the poor in the industrial age, and pioneer of the Monitorial school system. 1798: Set up the Borough Road School using the system of monitors to teach them. Supported by other Quakers, the system spread and by 1851, 826 British schools were established. Borough Road also became the earliest teacher training institution.

(Continued)

Table 1.1   (Continued)

Born	Died	Name	Summary of achievements
1782	1852	Friedrich Froebel	In 1826 published *The Education of Man* in which he argues for the importance of play in education. Froebel's ideas became influential in Britain around the mid nineteenth century.
1784	1857	James Buchanan	1814: Worked with Robert Owen in New Lanark to run the infant school. Though reported not to have been a good manager, he enjoyed working with children using methods that reflected 'progressive' infant school work.
1791	1866	Samuel Wilderspin	1820: After meeting James Buchanan took charge of the new Quaker Street Infant School in Spitalfields.
1793	1865	Elizabeth Mayo	1829: Wrote *Lessons with Objects* which claimed that by arranging and classifying objects and discovering their qualities the child would be stimulated to learn. This influenced elementary education throughout the rest of the nineteenth century, including some rote learning.
1798	1869	William Ewart	1850: Successfully introduced a bill to establish free public libraries supported from local rates.
1804	1877	Sir James Phillips Kay-Shuttleworth	1839–40: Established a training college at Battersea which became the model for nineteenth-century training of elementary school teachers.
1811	1892	Robert Lowe	Introduced the Revised Code in 1862 which included the introduction of 'payment results' whereby grants to elementary schools were based principally upon pupils' performances in annual examinations in reading, writing and arithmetic. 'Payment by Results' continued for 35 years until 1899.
1812	1870	Charles Dickens	Through his novels he drew attention to the poor social conditions which affected children and the importance of education.
1814	1897	Emily Anne Eliza Shirreff	Campaigned for education of girls and women. In 1875 became president of the Froebel Society (founded in 1874). She emphasised the importance of the proper training of kindergarten teachers.

Table 1.1

Born	Died	Name	Summary of achievements
1818	1886	William Edward Forster	1870 Elementary Education Act established school boards in areas where there was a lack of elementary school provision.
1825	1897	Anthony John Mundella	Member of the Hadow Committee and responsible with Lord Spencer for the Mundella Act which became known as the Education Act of 1880 which introduced universal compulsory education in England. The 'Mundella' Code of 1882 encouraged 'enlightened' teaching methods in schools and allowed for a variety of subjects in the curriculum.
1837	1931	Sir William Hart Dyke	Played a leading part in promoting and distributing the 1890 Education Code which paved the way for the ending of the system of 'Payment by Results'. 1891: Introduced the Free Education Bill, which opened up the way to provide free elementary education to children.
1840	1938	Sir James Crichton-Brown	1884: As Vice President of the Committee of Council on Education, investigated cases of alleged 'overpressure' in London schools caused by the demands of the Mundella Code.
1842	1923	Charlotte Mason	Headmistress of one of England's first infant schools at 22 years of age. Pestalozzi trained, she started the first infant school in the country and championed home education and play as being as important as lessons, with the key phrase 'education is an atmosphere'.
1850	1936	Edmond Gore Alexander Holmes	1911: Published *What Is and What Might Be: A Study of Education in General and Elementary Education in Particular*. This book condemned the formal, systematized, examination-ridden education system and advocated co-operation, self-expression and activity methods. Holmes also importantly, criticised the system of 'Payment by Results'.

(Continued)

Table 1.1   (Continued)

Born	Died	Name	Summary of achievements
1851	1920	Mary Augusta Ward (Mrs Humphry)	In 1890 founded centre for social work, bible teaching and 'children's play hours' at Gordon Square, London. The Children's Play Hours scheme led to establishment of recreational centres for London children, transferred to centres for London children, transferred to Tavistock Square in 1897, and became the Passmore Edwards Settlement. In 1898 Mary Ward began a scheme for 'crippled' children which contributed to the general recognition of the need for special resources and provision for some children.
1855	1931	Edward Parnell Culverwell	1913: Published *The Montessorian Principles and Practice* advocating modern, Montessorian teaching methods. Thus introducing the method to the UK.
1856	1936	Sigmund Freud	Developed an approach to psychoanalysis which provided a way of interpreting the behaviour of young children.
1859	1952	John Dewey	Promoted progressive and child-centred education through teaching based on integrated learning through projects rather than discreet subjects.
1859	1917	Rachel McMillan	1913: Established the Rachel McMillan Open-Air Nursery School in London, based on her ideas about preschool education with a large garden with shelters and other outdoor facilities. She focused particularly on work with children from slum areas.
1860	1931	Margaret McMillan	In 1899 Margaret McMillan participated in one of the first medical inspections of children under government auspices, before campaigning successfully for school medical inspections in 1902. 1913: With her sister Rachel she established Camp schools and a nursery school. She established the Rachel McMillan Training College in memory of her sister in 1930.
1860	1932	Catherine Isabella Dodd	1902: Opening of experimental elementary school and kindergarten based on new teaching methods.

Table 1.1

Born	Died	Name	Summary of achievements
1861	1925	Rudolf Steiner	Founded the Waldorf-Steiner Education movement. The first school opened in 1919 based on Steiner's Anthroposophical principles and promoting co-education for children based on imitation and example and Steiner's beliefs about child/human development and the parallel development of moral life and teaching.
1864	1933	Dame Maude Agnes Lawrence	School inspector and administrator. Became Chief Woman Inspector in 1905 when the Woman Inspectorate was set up. The six women, at first, inspected education of very young children and girls in elementary schools, mainly in domestic subjects.
1870	1952	Maria Montessori	In 1907 opened, in Rome, the first House of Childhood, for children living in tenement housing aged between 3 and 7 years. Montessori's work emphasised the importance of children's environments. She developed successful methods of working with children described as 'mentally defective'.
1872	1937	Edith Mary Deverell	1900: Appointed to the Inspectorate. Joined five other women inspectors who were inspecting girls' and infants' departments in elementary schools. Campaigned to secure the interest and co-operation of parents in the work of the school.
1882	1960	Melanie Klein	Psychoanalyst who employed 'free [therapeutic] play' techniques with children. In 1932 published *The Psychoanalysis of Children*. A pioneer of knowledge of the 'mental life' of infant children and an important influence on general attitudes to young children.
1883	1973	Alexander Sutherland (A. S.) Neill	In 1924 A. S. Neill founded his own school in Lyme Regis, which on moving to Suffolk became known as the famous Summerhill School, based on radically liberal, humanist and child-centred principles.
1885	1948	Susan Sutherland Isaacs	1924–27: Established the Malting House School, Cambridge, with a curriculum and pedagogy designed to further the *individual* development of children. Author of several books which include observations and reflections of children at the Malting House School. (Thus an early *systematic* researcher.)

(Continued)

Table 1.1   (Continued)

Born	Died	Name	Summary of achievements
1886	1939	Henry Caldwell Cook	1917: Published *The Play Way: An Essay in Educational Method.* Believed that the existing school system hampered 'true' education, arguing (as Dewey was to) that: 'Proficiency and learning come not from reading and listening but from action, from doing and from experience'.
1892	1946	Marion Richardson	Mostly influential as Inspector for Art during the 1930s in London. Influenced the teaching of handwriting during the late 1930s, with the publication of *Writing and Writing Patterns* (1935) which influenced the teaching of handwriting in primary schools.
1895	1976	Louis Christian Schiller	HMI, promoted child-centred learning and education through the arts. Worked closely with Robin Tanner running courses for serving teachers.
1896	1934	Lev Semenovich Vygotsky	Psychologist and educational theorist best known for his emphasis on learning as an act of social interaction and his theory of the 'Zone of Proximal Development'.
1896	1971	Donald Woods Winnicott	A paediatrician and psychoanalyst who developed a framework of human emotional development which supports the development of environments and practices to enable children to develop as secure and emotionally 'whole' human beings.
1896	1980	Jean Piaget	Psychologist who put forward stages of cognitive development which informed practice in early years teaching. Corresponded with Susan Isaacs.
1900	1969	Sir Fred Joyce Schonell	Most renowned for influence on primary school method of teaching – in particular, approaches to teaching children with learning difficulties. In 1944 wrote the *Happy Venture* reading scheme and developed the reading test of his name.
1901	1985	Sir James Pitman	Inventor of the Initial Teaching Alphabet (ita) – a simplified format to aid learning of reading which was in vogue in some schools during the 1960s but which did not become universally established infant teaching practice.

Table 1.1

Born	Died	Name	Summary of achievements
1902	1994	Erik Erikson	Psychologist and psychoanalyst whose theory of human development prompted the development of early childhood programmes which supported healthy social and emotional development.
1902	1987	Carl Rogers	Psychologist and psychotherapist who put forward an approach to education which was based on reciprocal relationships between children and between children and their teachers.
1904	1990	Burrhus Frederic (B. F.) Skinner	Psychologist who developed theory of behaviourism which promoted a system of learning which involved a 'stimulus-response' approach in order to modify undesirable behaviour.
1904	1988	Robin Tanner	Promoted the arts in education and ran courses for teachers with Christian Schiller at the Institute of Education in London.
1907	1990	John Bowlby	Psychoanalyst who is renowned for his 'Attachment' theory.
1909	1986	Sir Alec Clegg	Chief Education Officer of West Riding, Yorkshire 1945–74. Emphasising the importance of creativity in all educational processes, made key contributions to teachers' INSET and to the organisation and curricula of schools and settings. Made an extensive collection of children's artwork from West Riding schools 1930s–1974 and expounded the importance of creativity.
1910	1971	Sir John Hubert Newsom	Like Clegg, a pioneer of systematic development of school needs and processes. 1963: Chair of the Central Advisory Council on education which produced the Newsom Report, *Half Our Future,* reporting on education of 'average and below average' children. Deputy Chair of the Central Advisory Council, which produced, The Plowden Report, *Children and their Primary Schools* (1967). Wrote several books including *Willingly to School* (1944), *The Education of Girls* (1948) and *The Child at School* (1950).

Into the twenty-first century: twenty years of policy change

> How comes change? We read of its coming in the books of history – 'change was in the air', 'that was the decisive year', 'then came the breakthrough', but when we live through history it is quite different: change takes place on the ground not in the air, each year seems only too much like the next, and as for the breakthrough – we wait for it in vain. Yet, looking back over a period, somehow change has come. (Schiller 1979: 17)

Understanding recent history: 1998–2008

When we look back over these last few years, it seems that the slow and fitful development of early childhood education in the UK is now central to educational and social change. There has been something of an explosion of activity, a burgeoning of initiatives, interest and resources. Thus, in the last 20 years alone, from 1988 to 2008, there have been at least 20 major new policies (an average of one per year) which apart from their individual effects have, as a whole, changed the shape and status of early childhood education almost beyond recognition. A teacher recently told us: 'It's odd, I started teaching in 1988 and I've been looking back at old files and things and clearing out planning sheets, class lists, those kinds of things. Looking back I found myself plotting these 20 years almost exactly in terms of a policy a year!'

A brief survey of this period reveals how policy changes have involved early childhood educators in the following:

- the National Curriculum and subsequent revisions;
- rigorous and (sometimes) stressful inspection processes;
- the Children Act 1989;
- interpretation of expected 'desirable outcomes' of nursery education;
- new Codes of Practice for the identification of children with Special Educational Needs;
- changes in relation to national assessment of children on entry to school, known as 'Baseline Assessment';
- the National Childcare Strategy in 1998;
- working, during the 1990s, with diminishing resources followed by high profile, funded activity and increasing expectations during the 2000s;
- working with diminishing support and limited opportunities for professional development, followed by expectations of further qualifications and funded professional development;
- grappling with issues affecting the teaching of four-year-olds in school;
- Early Years Development and Childcare Partnerships (EYDCPs);
- working within a developing network of diversity of provision and EYDCPs;

- the National Literacy Strategy;
- the National Numeracy Strategy;
- new Foundation Stage curriculum developed from government guidance;
- transforming the Foundation Stage from policy to practice;
- the Foundation Stage Profile;
- *Every Child Matters* (2003)
- *The Ten Year Childcare Strategy* (2004);
- *Birth to Three Matters* Framework;
- the revised Early Years Foundation Stage (2007);
- acquiring Early Years Professional Status.

It is important to remember that this list is by no means exhaustive and, of course, is supplemented by other social and educational policies which have – equally, if less directly – impacted on the culture, structure and status of early childhood education. As well as these demanding policy shifts, recent years have seen the establishment of what might be called a new status for the early childhood workforce, with:

- unprecedented government investment;
- professional development opportunities (and expectations);
- networks of support;
- expectation of further qualifications of all staff working with children from birth to five.

Into the future, learning from the past

Learning from the past is one way of trying to ensure that new policies and investment do not repeat the mistakes of previous generations. We shall come to this later in the book where we examine the ways in which influential figures or deeds in the history and development of early childhood education the UK has helped to shape present-day policy and practice and serves to locate current experience within a history of ideas, beliefs and values. However, throughout the book it will become apparent that policy-makers do not always learn from the past and, as we shall see, ideas sometimes seem to return, are sometimes re-invented and appear in 'new clothes' but nevertheless bear distinctly familiar shapes (even if bringing new intentions).

The point of this examination of the work and thinking of people who have contributed to the development of early childhood education, is to try to understand how some of the most useful ideas can be drawn upon and developed. There is no 'history for the sake of history' here, rather a reflection on some of the lessons which might be learned in order to understand the present state of early childhood education and how it has come to be what it is.

2 The Pioneers: Their Lives and Works

> ... there have been great men and women whose vision and action have inspired a generation: Robert Owen, Friedrich Froebel, in our own time, Margaret McMillan and others. But they pass away, and their ideas pass away with them unless these ideas are fashioned into new forms which reflect new circumstances and stand the test of new practices in the contemporary scene. The pioneers take such ideas and refashion and temper them in their daily work in school. Patiently, day after day, week after week and year after year they make the pathway from the past through the present towards the future.
>
> (Schiller 1951: xvii)

In this part of the book we present a chronologically arranged series of biographies of 24 key figures who contributed as pioneers to the development of early childhood education through their work in: child development; philosophy; psychology; curriculum; pedagogy; social policy; and different forms of provision of early childhood education and care. We should emphasise that this is neither a systematic nor an exhaustive collection; rather, we have chosen pioneers in whose work we can see distinctive contributions to the development of early childhood education. Some of the names will be familiar (if not famous) and certainly widely acknowledged as 'pioneers' worthy of the name. But we believe that the less familiar names are no less to be seen as pioneers, even if their spheres of influence were smaller, local and less celebrated.

These brief biographies are intended as introductions to the people, their most important contributions to the early childhood field and their key writings. Those featured here have been chosen because some of them have influenced our own beliefs, research and practices and some were suggested by our students and other contemporary contributors to the field of early childhood education. It will be clear that some of the people we have included here have an obvious place, while for others their contribution and inclusion may be less immediately apparent. We do not claim a comprehensive 'who's who' – or 'who *was* who'! – in the history of early childhood, but those included here, we feel, provide a starting point for explorations of 'old' ideas.

How this section is used is a matter of reader preference. Some may wish to read it through chronologically, others may wish to refer to selected biographies. However, we suggest that before the conversations in Part 3 are read, the biographies of the people featured in them are consulted because they include important background material which further illuminates the conversations.

The Biographies

469–399 BC	Socrates
1592–1670	Jan Amos Komenský (Comenius)
1712–1778	Jean-Jacques Rousseau
1746–1827	Johann Heinrich Pestalozzi
1771–1858	Robert Owen
1782–1852	Friedrich Froebel
1812–1870	Charles Dickens
1824–1923	Charlotte Mason
1856–1936	Sigmund Freud
1859–1917	Rachel McMillan
1859–1952	John Dewey
1860–1931	Margaret McMillan
1861–1925	Rudolf Steiner
1870–1952	Maria Montessori
1883–1973	Alexander Sutherland (A. S.) Neill
1885–1948	Susan Sutherland Isaacs
1895–1976	Louis Christian Schiller
1896–1934	Lev Semenovich Vygotsky
1896–1971	Donald Woods Winnicott
1896–1980	Jean Piaget
1902–1994	Erik Erickson
1902–1987	Carl Rogers
1904–1990	Burrhus Frederic (B. F.) Skinner
1904–1988	Robin Tanner

Socrates

Born:	469 BC, Athens
Died:	399 BC, Athens
Personal details:	Son of Sophroniscus (thought to be a stonemason) and Phaenarete (a midwife). Married with children, he spent most of his life in Athens. He was executed for his lack of belief in Athens' gods and for corrupting the young.
Profession(s):	Socrates fought in the Greek army, and served on an executive council of the Greek Assembly.
Key contributions to early childhood education:	According to Plato's writings it is perhaps his idea of teaching through the learners' questions which is most useful to early childhood education. He emphasised the importance of philosophy and of talking with others about life's questions.
Key texts:	He wrote nothing himself; the main evidence of his thinking was recorded by his contemporaries, Plato and Xenophon.
Quotations:	'Wisdom begins in wonder.'
	'The unexamined life is not worth living for a human being.'
Biographies:	Kraut, R. (1984) *Socrates and the State*. Princeton, NJ: Princeton University Press.
	Penner, T. (1992) 'Socrates and the early dialogues', in R. Kraut, (ed.), *The Cambridge Companion to Plato*. Cambridge: Cambridge University Press.
	Santas, G. X. (1979) *Socrates: Philosophy in Plato's Early Dialogues*. London: Routledge and Kegan Paul.

Jan Amos Komenský (Comenius)

Born:

28 March 1592, in the southern part of Moravia (now the Czech Republic)

Died:

15 November 1670, Amsterdam, Netherlands. (His grave has been declared Czech soil by the Dutch government; thus, his desire to be buried in Czech soil was fulfilled.)

Personal details:

Orphaned at the age of 12, Comenius was eventually exiled by the outbreak of religious wars. He married twice, and both wives died as did his two sons. In 1628, Comenius settled in Lezno, Poland, where he wrote his first books advocating the reform of the education system. His whole library was lost in a fire. He is variously referred to as the 'Teacher of Nations' and the 'Father of Modern Education'.

Profession(s):

Comenius was educated at Heidelberg University, Germany and ordained a clergyman. He returned to Moravia to become a schoolmaster and church pastor at Fulnek.

Key contributions to early childhood education:

His books, *The Great Didactic* and *The School of Infancy*, proposed that education should not be limited to the action of the school and family but is part of general social life. He believed that teachers should understand how a child's mind develops and that all children should receive the same education, whatever their gender and social class. He promoted education that was 'thorough, natural and enjoyable' and opposed rote learning.

He visited England in 1641 and worked in Sweden and Hungary to reform school systems.

Orbis Sensualium Pictus, published in 1658, is believed to be the first illustrated textbook for children.

He was greatly respected by many in seventeenth-century Europe but less popular with some figures who are thought to have been responsible for his name being absent from any history of philosophy for two centuries.

Key texts:

The School of Infancy (1631)
The Great Didactic (1657)
Orbis Sensualium Pictus (1658)

Quotations:

'Teach gently so that neither the teacher nor the pupils feel any difficulties or dislike; on the contrary, both find it very pleasant. And teach thoroughly, not super-ficially, but bring everyone to a real education, noble manners and devout piety.' (*The Great Didactic*, 1657)

Biographies:

Laurie, S. S. (1904) *John Amos Comenius, Bishop of Moravians: His Life and Educational Works* (6th edn). Cambridge: Cambridge University Press.

Murphy, D. J. (1995) *Comenius: A Critical Reassessment of his Life and Work*. Dublin: Irish Academic Press.

Spinka, M. (1967) *John Amos Comenius: That Incomporable Moravian* (2nd edn). New York: Russell and Russell.

Jean-Jacques Rousseau

Born: 1712, Geneva

Died: 2 July 1778, Ermenonville, near Paris

Personal details: Son of a watchmaker whose mother died days after his birth, Rousseau had little formal education. He lived with Thérèse Levasseur and had five children whom he left to an orphanage. Later this was used by those who opposed his theories on education and child care to attack him. Rousseau's writings were controversial and he eventually fled to and settled in Paris where his ideas continued to attract attention and criticism.

Profession(s): He became an apprentice and then an engraver. Between 1740 and 1741 he was private tutor to two sons of a French nobleman, then moved to Paris in 1742. From 1743 to 1744, he was secretary to the French ambassador in Venice. Rousseau pursued his interest in music and in 1752 his opera *Le Devin du Village* was performed for King Louis XV.

Key contributions to early childhood education: Rousseau is best known for *Emile*, his work on developmental psychology and implications for education. In *Emile*, Rousseau details the growth of a young boy under his care. In this largely fictional work, Emile grows up in what Rousseau saw as the natural setting for a child – the countryside – where his education is designed to help him learn how to live. Rousseau discusses Emile's development in three stages: up to 12 (a period which Rousseau characterised as more animal like); 12 to 16 (the beginning of reasoned thought); and 16 onwards (the beginning of adulthood).

Emile sets out Rousseau's ideals for living. The boy is protected from bad influences while he learns how to follow his instincts and think for himself. It is education designed by Rousseau for a boy, and this is not what he would have proposed for a girl, who would be taught to obey.

Emile has been criticised for being impractical, and Rousseau was aware of much of the criticism which was attracted by his ideas and made it clear that *Emile* was an ideal, not a reality; a philosophical position rather than a 'true treatise on education'.

Key texts:

Discourse on the Arts and Sciences (1750)
Emile: or, On Education (1762)
The Social Contract (1762)

Quotations:

'The strongest is never strong enough to be always the master, unless he transforms strength into right, and obedience into duty.' (Rousseau, 1762)

'Man is born free, but everywhere he is in chains.' (Rousseau, 1762)

'The training of children is a profession, where we must know how to waste time in order to save it.' (Rousseau, 1762)

'The person who has lived the most is not the one with the most years but the one with the richest experiences.' (Rousseau, 1750)

Biographies and commentries:

Bertram, C. (2003) *Rousseau and 'The Social Contract'*. London: Routledge.

Cooper, L. (1999) *Rousseau, Nature and the Problem of the Good Life*. University Part, PA: Pennsylvania State University Press.

Cranston, M. (1982) *Jean-Jacques: The Early Life and Work*. New York: Norton.

Damrosch, L. (2005) *Jean-Jacques Rousseau: Restless Genius*. New York: Houghton Mifflin.

Dent, N. J. H. (1988) *Rousseau: An Introduction to his Psychological, Social, and Political Theory*. Oxford: Blackwell.

Dent, N. J. H. (2005) *Rousseau*. London: Routledge.

Lange, L. (2002) *Feminist Interpretations of Jean-Jacques Rousseau*. University Park, PA: Pennsylvania State University Press.

Wokler, R. (1995) *Rousseau*. Oxford: Oxford University Press.

See also the Rousseau Association: http://www.rousseau association.org

Johann Heinrich Pestalozzi

Born: 12 January 1746, Zurich, Switzerland

Died: 17 February 1827, Brugg, Switzerland

Personal details: Pestalozzi had Italian Protestant roots and was from a middle-class family. His father was a surgeon and oculist who died when Pestalozzi was young and the family then lived under less affluent circumstances. He is said to have had a happy childhood, his mother influencing his thinking about how young children should spend their early years, playing and enjoying family activities. He married at 23 and first tried farming as a livelihood.

At the University of Zurich he became part of the political reform party working to improve conditions for ordinary people. He later focused his work on education.

In 1798 the French invaded Switzerland and Pestalozzi rescued several children who had been abandoned on the shores of Lake Lucerne and cared for them personally, in a disused convent, until the French claimed the building in 1799.

Profession(s):   Pedagogue and educational reformer.

Key contributions to early childhood education: His early educational experiments were unsuccessful but he opened a school in his farmhouse, and in 1801 published *How Gertrude Teaches her Children*, a book that influenced pedagogical thinking of the period. In it he explained his ideas for a form of instruction that was in line with the laws of nature. Children should learn through activity, through things rather than words, and be free to pursue their own interests and draw their own conclusions. Putting some of Rousseau's ideas into practice, his major contribution to education came towards the latter part of his life, when, from 1804, he spent 20 years at Yverdon. He and his wife established an educational institute for poor and underprivileged children. Some 150 boys (aged between 7 and 15 years) were cared for and educated according to each of their needs. In 1806 a similar school for girls was established, and in 1813 the first school in Switzerland for children with hearing and/or speech difficulties opened. Social scientists of the time were greatly interested in the Pestalozzi philosophy and practices. His work was not easy and not all the teachers agreed on how things should be done. Around 1815 there were difficulties with the teachers and he struggled to maintain the schools as he believed they should be until his retirement in 1825.

While his schools were important achievements, his most important contribution was in the principles of education which he established and demonstrated: observation; an interest in the 'whole' person; and the sympathetic approach of teachers. Key themes in his work are a refusal to allow 'method' to dominate what teachers did and a reluctance to make young children conform to views of what was 'correct'.

Pestalozzi saw education as central to the improvement of social conditions and believed that schools could play an important role. Victorian reformers took up his vision for education as the cornerstone of welfare policy through the nineteenth and twentieth centuries.

Key texts:

How Gertrude Teaches her Children: An Attempt to Help Mothers to Teach Their Own Children (1801)
Help for Teaching Spelling, and Reading (1801)
'Pestalozzi's Elementary Books' (1803) – six short books: three on *Intuitive-instruction in the Relations of Number;* two on *Intuitive-instruction in the Relations of Dimensions;* and one entitled *The Mother's Manual or Guide to Mothers in Teaching their Children How to Observe and Think.*

Quotations:

'The wish to be acquainted with some branches of knowledge that took hold of my heart and my imagination even though I neglected the means of acquiring them, was, nevertheless, enthusiastically alive within me, and, unfortunately, the tone of public instruction in my native town at this period was in a high degree calculated to foster this visionary fancy of taking an active interest in, and believing oneself capable of, the practice of things in which one had by no means had sufficient exercise.' (Pestalozzi, 1801)

'... life for the young child should be happy and free, and education in self-control should be gradual and careful. Punishment and restraint should rarely be necessary. Pressure to learn beyond the child's natural pace is harmful, and the denying of opportunities to learn by trial and error retards the development of character as well as of learning.' (Pestalozzi, 1801)

Biographies:

Biber, G. E. (1831) *Henry Pestalozzi and his Plan of Education.* London: John Souter, School Library.
Silber, K. (1960) *Pestalozzi: The Man and his Work.* London: Routledge and Kegan Paul.

Robert Owen

Born: 14 May 1771, Newtown, Montgomeryshire

Died: 1858

Personal details: Owen's father (also Robert Owen) was a saddler, ironmonger and postmaster. His mother, Anne Williams, had seven children, of which Owen was the sixth child. He developed an early love of reading. At the age of nine Robert Owen worked as a grocery boy and when he was ten he worked with his brother in London doing saddlery. He married Ann Dale, daughter of David Dale who owned the mills at New Lanark, in 1799.

Profession(s):   In 1790 Owen went into business manufacturing yarn. Later, he managed a large Manchester fabric mill before moving to manage the New Lanark mills in 1800. Owen refused to employ pauper children in the mills and promoted a standard for community living in New Lanark mill homes which included sanitation, education and what were considered to be less exploitative working conditions. He also insisted that good behaviour of employees was rewarded.

Key contributions to early childhood education: Owen limited the working hours of children in the mills by his involvement of the Factory Act of 1819. Children under ten were not employed in the mills, and instead went to school.

His clear enjoyment and liking for children showed in his views of how they should be treated in school; he strongly opposed corporal punishment and rewarded cleanliness and good conduct. He insisted that his teachers treated pupils well and did not instil fear of them but promoted a love of reading and learning.

Key texts: *A New View of Society and Other Writings* (1812)

Quotations: '[There is] something fundamentally wrong with all religions.'

'The object is no less than to remove gross ignorance and extreme poverty, with their attendant misery, from your population, and to make it rational, well disposed, and well behaved.' (*Glasgow Herald*, 20 April 1812)

'… human nature is radically good, and is capable of being trained, educated, and placed from birth in such manner, that all ultimately … must become united, good, wise, wealthy, and happy.' (Owen 1920: 181)

Biographies: Owen, R. (1920) *The Life of Robert Owen: Written by Himself*. London: G. Bell and Sons.

Friedrich Froebel

Born: 21 April 1782, Oberweissbach, Saxony (now Germany)

Died: 21 June 1852, Marienthal, Saxony

Personal details: Froebel was born into a clergyman's family. His mother died when he was only nine months old, and he was neglected as a child until an uncle gave him a home and sent him to school. Upon leaving school he served an apprenticeship to a forester, furthering his knowledge of natural phenomena and his love of plants.

Profession(s):   Froebel taught at a progressive school in Frankfurt that was run on the lines advocated by Johann Heinrich Pestalozzi where he became convinced of his vocation as a teacher and after two years went to teach at Yverdon in Switzerland under Pestalozzi.

He opened his own school with a colleague and settled at Keilhau in 1818. It was here that Froebel began to put many of his educational theories into practice in the school that took the form of an educational community.

Key contributions to early childhood education: In 1826 Froebel published his most important work, *The Education of Man*.

In 1831 he accepted the Swiss government's invitation to train elementary school teachers, at which time he became convinced of the importance of the early stages of education.

He returned to Keilhau in 1837 and opened an infant school, which he eventually named the Kindergarten or 'Garden of children'.

Froebel started a publishing business for play and other educational materials to stimulate learning through well-directed play activities accompanied by songs and music. His experiments at the Kindergarten attracted widespread interest – especially the use of 'gifts' (play materials) and 'occupations' (activities) – and other kindergarten schools soon became established.

Froebel's ideas were soon brought to the notice of educators in England, France and the Netherlands and eventually the United States where they became a cornerstone of standard educational provision for children from four to six years of age.

Key texts:

The Education of Man (Die Menschenerziehung) (1826)
Mother Songs (Mutter und Koselieder) (1843)

Quotations:

'The purpose of education is to encourage and guide man as a conscious, thinking and perceiving being in such a way that he becomes a pure and perfect representation of that divine inner law through his own personal choice; education must show him the ways and meanings of attaining that goal.' (Froebel 1826: 2)

Biographies:

Kilpatrick, W. H. (1916) *Froebel's Kindergarten Principles Critically Examined.* New York: Macmillan.
Lawrence, E. (ed.) (1952) *Friedrich Froebel and English Education.* London: University of London Press. Series of essays on key elements of Froebel's thought and practice.

Charles Dickens

Born: 7 February 1812, Portsmouth

Died: 9 June 1870, Gad's Hill

Personal details: Dickens worked from 1827 to 1832 in a solicitors' office and as a law-court reporter. He was a parliamentary reporter from 1832 to 1836. He began writing stories in 1833. He had nine children.

Profession(s):   He is best known as a novelist.

Key contributions to early childhood education: Dickens' concerns around education arise in his writing about society and crime. His ideas about education of the poor appear to stem from a view of crime prevention. He became involved in Ragged Schools from 1843, and drew attention to social issues and the effects of poverty on children through his novels and in his letters. The kindergarten movement was first mentioned by Dickens in a letter written on 1 February 1855.

Key texts: Numerous novels but perhaps most relevant to early childhood are:
Nicholas Nickleby (1839)
David Copperfield (1850)
Bleak House (1852)
Hard Times (1854)
Great Expectations (1861)

Quotations: To teachers of the Ragged Schools: 'Good intentions alone will never be sufficient qualification for such a labour, while this world lasts.' (Dickens, in Collins, 1963: 138)

'I think it is right that the State should educate the people; and I think it is wrong that it should punish ignorance, without enlightening or preventing it. ... But I would limit its power and watch it very carefully. ... I apprehend that there are certain sound rudiments of a good education, and certain moral and religious truths, on which we might agree. I would have those taught in State Schools, to the children of parents of all Christian denominations, favouring no one Church more than another.' (Letter to Edward Baines, 7 June 1850, in Collins 1963: 52)

'Little Red Riding Hood was my first love. I felt that if I could have married Little Red Riding Hood, I should have known perfect bliss.' (Dickens in Bettleheim, 1988: 23)

Biographies:

Collins, P. (1963) *Dickens and Education*. London: Macmillan.

Hughes, J. L. (1900) *Dickens as an Educator*. New York: D. Appleton.

Manning, J. (1956) *Dickens on Education*. Toronto: University of Toronto Press.

Charlotte Mason

Born: 1 January 1842, Bangor

Died: 16 January 1923, Ambleside

Personal details: Charlotte Mason was an only child, from a reasonably affluent family. Her father was a Liverpool merchant and she was educated by her parents at home. Her mother died when she was 16 years old and her father when she was 17. She lived with friends until she was 18 when, in 1860, she moved to London to train at the first teacher training college, The Home and Colonial School Society established by Elizabeth and Charles Mayo who used the ideas of Pestalozzi.

Mason endured ill-health and suffered a breakdown which forced her to take breaks from her work. She travelled widely and wrote travel books as well as education books.

Profession(s):   Mason became headmistress of the Davison School for Infants in 1861, before she was fully trained. She was later to be Mistress of Method at Bishop Otter College, Chichester. She opened the House of Education in 1892, a women's teacher training college. The House of Education was renamed Charlotte Mason College and later became part of St Martin's College, Lancaster – now the University of Cumbria.

Key contributions to early childhood education: Drawing on the work of Rousseau and Pestalozzi, Charlotte Mason promoted education for girls and women. She promoted the use of the senses in learning and of learning through experiences and the outdoors.

She developed a clear and distinctive philosophy and wrote 20 articles on education which became known by some as a child's Bill of Rights. She established a teacher training college in Ambleside in 1892 which also had a Parents' Union School, where young children could attend, without charge, if their parents subscribed to the monthly *Parents' Review* journal that Charlotte Mason published to promote her work on home education through her home education network, the Parents' National Education Union.

Her promotion of parents as educators and home education makes her a key figure in the home education movement in the twenty-first century.

Key texts:

The Home Schooling Series:
Volume 1: Home Education. The education and training of children under nine (1886)
Volume 2: Parents and Children. A practical study of educational principles (1896)
Volume 3: Home and School Education. The training of education of children over nine (1904)
Volume 4: Ourselves, Our Souls and Bodies. Book 1: Self knowledge. Book 2: Self direction (1904)
Volume 5: Some Studies in the Formation of Character (1905)
An Essay Towards a Philosophy of Education (1923)

Quotations:

'It stultifies the child to bring down his world to the "child's level" '. (Mason 1923)

'... my object is to show that the chief function of the child – his business in the world during the first six or seven years of life – is to find out all he can, about whatever comes under his notice, by means of his five senses; that he has an insatiable appetite for knowledge got in this way; and that the endeavour of his parents should be to put him in the way of making acquaintance freely with nature and natural objects.' (Mason 1886: 96–7)

'Children have a right to the best we possess; therefore their lesson books should be, as far as possible, our best books.' (Mason 1923)

Sigmund Freud

Born: 6 May 1856, Freiberg, (now Příbor) (Czech Republic)

Died: 1936

Personal details: His father Jacob was 41 and his mother 21 when Freud was born to a family which eventually totalled 8 children. In 1859 he moved to Vienna with his family and in 1873 graduated from secondary school able to read in several languages. He then studied medicine at Vienna University. His early career involved him in research in psychiatry and neurology. After military service in 1880, he rejected medical practice in favour of research and teaching, but nevertheless graduated with a degree in medicine in 1881. He began psychiatric work in 1883 and treated 'nervous' disorders by 'electrotherapy' before developing work on hypnosis in 1885. He married in 1886 and had six children. He spent much of his life in Vienna until the Nazis annexed Austria in 1937 and Freud, being Jewish, left for England where he died of cancer in 1939.

Profession(s):   Freud was a medical doctor specialising in physiology and psychology. He is known as the 'father' of psychoanalysis, and was a highly influential thinker of his time who put forward concepts of the unconscious, infantile sexuality and repression of experiences. He developed a radically new approach to the analysis and understanding of the human mind. His work on the interpretation of dreams and the role of subconscious symbolism is still influential in many aspects of life and work today.

Key contributions   Freud's theory on infantile sexuality and the 'Oedipus
to early childhood   complex' has been used to interpret the behaviour of
education: young children.
                       His identification of three structural elements in the mind, *id*, *ego*, and *super-ego*, has been used to understand and interpret children's behaviour.

Key texts: *The Standard Edition of the Complete Psychological Works of Sigmund Freud*, 24 vols (1953–64).

Quotations: 'My life is interesting only if is related to psychoanalysis.'

'When you were incontestably the favourite child of your mother, you keep during your lifetime this victor feeling, you keep feeling sure of success, which in reality seldom doesn't fulfill.' (Freud 1917: 145)

Biographies: Bettelheim, B. (1982) *Freud and Man's Soul*. New York: Knopf.

Frosh, S. (1987) *The Politics of Psychoanalysis: An Introduction to Freudian and Post-Freudian Theory*. London and New Haven, CT: Yale University Press.

Jones, E. (1953–57) *Sigmund Freud: Life and Work* (3 vols). New York: Basic Books.

Wallace, E. R. (1983) *Freud and Anthropology: A History and Reappraisal*. International Universities Press.

Wollheim, R. (1971) *Freud*. London: Fontana.

Rachel McMillan

Born: 25 March 1859, New York

Died: 25 March 1917, London

Personal details: Following the death of her father and sister Elizabeth, she returned to Scotland with her mother and sister Margaret in 1865. On the death of her mother Jean McMillan in 1877, Rachel took over the care of her very sick grandmother. She became a Christian Socialist in 1887 and on the death of her grandmother in 1888 joined her sister Margaret in London, where she became a house mother in a home for girls in Bloomsbury. Rachel lived with Margaret for the rest of their lives. Rachel attended socialist meetings and wrote for the magazine *Christian Socialist*. Aware of the relationship between workers' physical environment and their intellectual development, Rachel and Margaret moved to Bradford in 1892 where they promoted Christian Socialism and visited the poor. Politically aware and active, they supported the campaign for universal suffrage but not the extreme actions of the Women's Social and Political Union.

Profession(s): Rachel McMillan was a political campaigner and health worker. She developed nursery provision for children of poor families as a means of promoting healthier lives.

Key contributions to early childhood education: In 1902 in London, Rachel worked closely with leaders of the movement including James Keir Hardie and George Lansbury to campaign for school meals, because they believed that hungry children could not learn, and her work was instrumental in the passing of the School Meals Act in 1906. In 1908 Rachel and Margaret McMillan opened the first school clinic and a 'Night Camp' where children living in the slums of London could wash and put on clean nightclothes. In 1914 their Open-Air Nursery School and Training Centre was opened in Peckham, for 30 children aged from 18 months to 7 years. Rachel was mainly responsible for the kindergarten and her sister worked on health issues.

Key texts:	Rachel was not the writer in the family; her sister Margaret was responsible for writing and publishing their ideas and work.
Quotations:	'I think that, very soon, when these teachings and ideas are better known, people generally will declare themselves Socialists.' (in McMillan, M. 1927)
Biographies:	McMillan, M. (1927) *The Life of Rachel McMillan.* London: J. M. Dent.

John Dewey

Born: 1859, Vermont

Died: 1952, New York

Personal details: Dewey came from a family of Vermont farmers. He graduated in philosophy from the University of Vermont and gained a PhD in 1884 before teaching and later becoming professor of philosophy at the University of Michigan. He married Alice Chipman in 1886 and moved to the University of Chicago in 1894 and then to Columbia University, New York, in 1904.

Profession(s):   Philosopher, educationalist and university professor.

Key contributions   His ideas on the contribution education might make
to early childhood   to alleviate social problems have pervaded many early
education: education programmes.

The Dewey Laboratory School became a well-established centre for 'progressive education' which employed a pedagogy based on ideas of democracy and child centredness. What became known as the 'project method' involved teachers and children working on ideas and finding solutions to questions. Dewey was critical of misinterpretations of these ideas: 'Many so-called projects are of such a short time-span and are entered upon for such casual reasons, that extension of aquaintance with facts and principles is at a minimum. In short, they are too trivial to be educative' (Dewey 1931: 31). The projects did not falsely divide knowledge into subjects but encouraged a more holistic approach to learning. The role of the teacher was to ensure that children's project ideas were realisable and to offer help and teaching at all stages where needed and where opportunities for teaching arose.

Dewey promoted (as did Vygotsky and Montessori) ideas of child-centred education, of activity and interaction, of education as a part of the social world of children and their communities.

Key texts:

Experience and Education (1897)
How We Think (1897)
My Pedagogic Creed (1897)
The School and Society (1899)

Quotations:

'… the fundamental issue is not of new versus old education nor of progressive against traditional education but a question of what, if anything whatever, must be worthy of the name Education.' (Dewey 1897)

'I believe that education … is a process of living, not a preparation for future living.' (Dewey 1897)

Biographies:

Tanner, L. N. (1997) *Dewey's Laboratory School: Lessons for Today*. New York: Teachers College Press.

Margaret McMillan

Born: 20 July 1860, New York

Died: 29 March 1931, London

Personal details: Margaret McMillan returned to Scotland with her mother and sister Rachel in 1865 following the death of her father and sister Elizabeth from scarlet fever, from which she had suffered herself resulting in deafness until the age of 14.

In 1887 after the death of her mother, Margaret went to London to train as a governess. From 1888 Margaret and Rachel lived and worked together for the rest of their lives. She was converted by her sister Rachel to socialism and attended political meetings. Margaret gave free evening lessons to working-class girls in London and became aware of the connection between working and living conditions and the capacity to learn.

Rachel and Margaret moved to Bradford in 1892 where they promoted Christian Socialism and visited the poor. Margaret McMillan, was elected Independent Labour Party member for the Bradford School Board in 1894, thus influencing work in Bradford schools.

Profession(s):   She was a suffragist and campaigner for nursery education and health care for young children.

Key contributions to early childhood education: Margaret was responsible for establishing medical inspections in elementary schools, and pioneered, with her sister Rachel, the first open-air nursery for under fives, where disadvantaged children could enjoy 'light, air and all that is good' (McMillan 1917).

When Rachel McMillan died on 25 March 1917, Margaret continued to run the Peckham Nursery which they had opened together. She also served on the London County Council and wrote several books. Margaret McMillan became interested in nursing, and in 1930 she established a college in Deptford to train teachers and nurses which was named the Rachel McMillan College.

Key texts:

Child Labour and the Half Time System (1896)
Early Childhood (1900)
The Camp School (1917)
The Nursery School (1919)
Nursery Schools: A Practical Handbook (1920)
Childhood, Culture, and Class in Britain (1925)

Quotations:

'Our mother was possessed by one aim – to give us children a proper education. She spared nothing in the pursuit of this end. The first experience of school was a little disconcerting and in some ways even alarming. The children sat in a large room with a desk that looked like a pulpit. This desk contained, as we afterwards learned with horror, a tawse, or leathern strap, with four tongues, which the masters used with energy, not indeed for the punishment of girls, but only of boys. In spite of our immunity, we were filled with anxiety and distress, and had a deep sympathy with the unruly boys.' (McMillan 1927)

'The condition of the poorer children was worse than anything that was described or painted. It was a thing that this generation is glad to forget. The neglect of infants, the utter neglect almost of toddlers and older children, the blight of early labour, all combined to make of a once vigorous people a race of undergrown and spoiled adolescents; and just as people looked on at the torture two hundred years ago and less, without any great indignation, so in the 1890s people saw the misery of poor children without perturbation.' (ibid.)

Rudolf Steiner

Born: 1861

Died: 1925

Personal details: Rudolf Steiner was Austrian. He founded *Anthroposophy* meaning – in Greek – 'Wisdom of Man'. Anthroposophy is a way of looking at one's whole life in connection with the spirit. For many Steiner-educated pupils, Steiner teachers and parents of children in Steiner schools, Anthroposophy is a way of life, not just a basis for a system of education.

Profession(s):   A scientist and a philosopher, in later life Steiner was greatly concerned with social issues which were the foundation of the Steiner-Waldorf school movement which, some 80 years after his death, is still active internationally and offers a comprehensive, socially inclusive co-educational alternative to State education systems in many countries.

Key contributions   Rudolf Steiner conceived of education as an art –
to early childhood   creative, progressive, social and individual. Teaching
education: is essentially vocational, a challenging yet fulfilling task, and teachers, in common with their pupils, remain learners. Not limited to schooling, teaching and learning mean taking one's place in the world, working with enthusiasm, acting with consideration, involving oneself responsibly (http://www. steiner-waldorf.org. uk/teaching.htm). Now an international movement, Steiner-Waldorf kindergartens are found in many countries, with over 40 in the UK. These kindergartens are early childhood settings which follow pedagogical practices based on the anthropo-sophical work of Rudolf Steiner. Steiner-Waldorf kindergartens are immediately recognisable for their homely characteristics. Furniture is often wooden, and the equipment available for the children is made of natural materials. Plastic toys are not a feature in Steiner kindergartens.[1]

---

[1] Steiner education http://www.steinerwaldorf.org.uk/teaching

The first Waldorf school was opened in 1919 with funding from the Waldorf Astoria company. Emil Molt, co-founder of the first school, wrote:

> I felt the tragedy of the working class: to be held back by lack of money from sharing the education of the rich middle class. I also had a sense of what it would mean for social progress if we could support a new educational endeavour within our factory ... (Molt 1919: 3)

The first Waldorf kindergarten was opened in 1926, the year after Steiner died. It was developed and run under the direction of Elizabeth von Grunelius, a teacher who had worked closely with Steiner in defining what kindergarten education in a Steiner school should look like. The Waldorf plan for early childhood education was published in *Educating the Young Child* (Grunelius 1974) in England in 1955 and set out the underpinning structures of Steiner-Waldorf kindergarten provision which were built upon *imitation* and *example*.

Key texts:	*The Study of Man* (1947) *Rudolf Steiner: An Autobiography* (1980) *The Kingdom of Childhood: Introductory Talks on Waldorf Education* (1995) – seven lectures and answers to questions, given in Torquay, 12–20 August 1924 *The Foundations of Human Experience* (1996) originally published as *The Study of Man* 1947
Quotations:	'The child has fantasy, and this fantasy is what we must engage. It is really a question of developing the concept of a kind of "milk for the soul".' (The Kingdom of Childhood, p. 14) 'You must teach and educate out of the very nature of the human being, and for this reason education for moral life must run parallel to the actual teaching ...' (ibid.: 52)
Biographies and commentaries:	Aeppli, W. (1986) *Rudolf Steiner Education and the Developing Child*. Hudson, NY: Anthroposophic Press.

Lissau, R. (1987) *Rudolf Steiner: Life, Work, Inner Path and Social Initiatives*. Stroud: Hawthorn Press.

Murphy, C. (1991) *Emil Molt and the Beginnings of the Waldorf School Movement*. Edinburgh: Floris Books.

Oldfield, L. (2001) *Free to Learn: Introducing Steiner-Waldorf Early Childhood Education*. Stroud: Hawthorn Press. Provides a clear discussion of Steiner-Waldorf pedagogy and several examples illustrate aspects of this work.

Maria Montessori

Born: 31 August 1870, Chiaravalle, Italy

Died: 6 May 1952, The Netherlands

Personal details: Maria Montessori graduated from technical school in 1886, where she was a very bright student. She studied modern languages and natural sciences. From 1886 to 1890 she attended Regio Instituto Tecnico Leonardo da Vinci.

She had one son, Mario Montessori, in 1898. Montessori had a love affair with her colleague, Dr Montesano, but they never married. Montessori was exiled by Mussolini mostly because she refused to compromise her principles and make the children into soldiers.

Profession(s):   Maria Montessori was an Italian medical doctor who worked with children with learning difficulties in socially deprived areas of Rome. In 1907 she began work with 50 children living in the slum areas of Rome who, within two years, were considered to be achieving educationally alongside other children of their age. Her success brought her world-wide acclaim. Her first 'Casa dei Bambini' (Children's house or household) was opened in Rome in 1907.

While well known for her distinctive work on early childhood curriculum and pedagogy, Maria Montessori was well respected in the world of science, being invited to the US in 1915 by Alexander Graham Bell and Thomas Edison to address an audience at Carnegie Hall. She was politically active and her expression of anti-fascist views forced her into exile during the Second World War. She was twice nominated for the Nobel Peace Prize and – until the adoption by Italy of the euro – her face appeared on the 1,000 lire note, in recognition and honour of her achievements.

Key contributions to early childhood education: From her early work, Montessori developed a set of principles, based on her observation of these children, which she argues were applicable to the learning of all children. The 'Montessori Method' is based on a phi-losophy which encompasses a range of issues, namely: multi-age grouping of children according to periods of development; human tendencies; the process of chil-dren's learning; the prepared environment; observa-tion; work centres; teaching method; class size; basic lessons; areas of study; daily schedule; assessment; learning styles; and character education.

Within these many elements the notion of 'human tendencies' is perhaps key. Montessori developed her methods by building on her observations that learn-ing is brought about by human tendencies to do – to act, to explore, to create. She observed that learning happened through repetition, concentration, imagi-nation, and that learners needed to be independent in their actions while making their own decisions about what 'work' they should do and learning how to con-trol their own actions.

Between 1907 and the mid 1930s, Maria Montessori dedicated herself to the development of schools throughout Europe and North America. From around 1935 to 1947 she worked in India and Sri Lanka, train-ing teachers in the Montessori curriculum and method.

Montessori was, undoubtedly, a pioneer in the field of child care and education and, though famous for her influence on early childhood education, her work included ways of working with children of all ages. Montessorian approaches are used internation-ally in education settings and in home-based provi-sion for children.

Key texts:

Dr Montessori's Own Handbook (1914)
Education for a New World (1962)
The Secret of Childhood (1963)
The Absorbent Mind (1964)
The Montessori Method (1964)

Quotations:

'Like others I had believed that it was necessary to encourage a child by means of some exterior reward that would flatter his baser sentiments, such as gluttony, van-ity, or self-love, in order to foster in him a spirit of work and peace. And I was astonished when I learned that a child who is permitted to educate himself really gives up these lower instincts. I then urged the teachers to cease handing out the ordinary prizes and punishments, which were no longer suited to our children, and to confine themselves to directing them gently in their work.' (Montessori 1964)

'We should really find the way to teach the child how, before making him execute a task.' (Montessori 1964)

Biographies: Kramer, R. (1976) *Maria Montessori*. Toronto: Longman Canada Limited.

Alexander Sutherland (A. S.) Neill

Born:	17 October 1883, Forfar, Scotland
Died:	23 September 1973
Personal details:	Neill's father was a teacher, and Neill became a pupil-teacher in his father's school. In 1912, he graduated with an MA from the University of Edinburgh. By 1914 he was headmaster of the Gretna Green School in Scotland. Neill married twice; his second wife Ena Wood Neill administered Summerhill School until 1985, when their daughter, Zoe Neill Readhead, took over the school as headmistress.
Profession(s):	Neill was a progressive educator, author and founder of Summerhill School, which remains open and continues to follow his educational philosophy to this day. He is best known as an advocate of personal freedom for children.
Key contributions to early childhood education:	Neill's ideas of freedom in education were highly controversial in their time. However, his work influenced many progressive educators who came after him. Perhaps the main influence on the early years was an ethos of respect for children and a fluid approach to learning and curriculum. The central tenet of Neill's philosophy was the freedom of the child and the resistance to oppressive routines and regimes.
Key texts:	*A Dominie's Log* (1916) *The Last Man Alive* (1939) *Summerhill: A Radical Approach to Child Rearing* (1960) *Neill, Neill, Orange Peel!* (1973)
Quotations:	'[I am] … just enough of a Nietzschian to protest against teaching children to be meek and lowly.' (Neill 1960) '[I am] trying to form minds that will question and destroy and rebuild.' (ibid.) 'The function of the child is to live his own life – not the life that his anxious parents think he should live,

nor a life according to the purpose of the educator who thinks he knows best.' (ibid.)

'No one is wise enough or good enough to mould the character of any child. What is wrong with our sick, neurotic world is that we have been moulded, and an adult generation that has seen two great wars and seems about to launch a third should not be trusted to mould the character of a rat.' (ibid.)

Biographies:

Croall, J. (1983) *Neill of Summerhill: The Permanent Rebel.* London: Routledge and Kegan Paul.

Walmsley, J. (1969) *Neill and Summerhill: A Pictorial Study.* Baltimore, MD: Penguin.

Susan Sutherland Isaacs

Born: 24 May 1885, near Bolton, Lancashire

Died: 12 October 1948, London

Personal details: Susan Sutherland Isaacs was the last of nine children, whose mother died when she was six. Her own schooling was difficult and she was removed from school at the age of 14 although she continued to self-educate vigorously.

Profession(s):   Isaacs trained and practised as a psychoanalyst and such training and experience clearly influenced her work, particularly with regard to observing young children's behaviour. Isaacs trained as a teacher and in 1912 obtained an Honours degree in philosophy and a scholarship to Cambridge. After two lecturing posts she founded the experimental Malting House School, Cambridge, in 1924.

Key contributions to early childhood education: The Malting House School had an experimental philosophy with no fixed curriculum and placed an emphasis on individual development and joy in discovery.

For Isaacs, children quite naturally experience intense feelings of fear, hate, jealousy and guilt, and she argued that they should have the freedom to express them in a free yet carefully contained environment.

In 1930 she published *Intellectual Growth in Young Children* and three years later *Social Development in Young Children*. During the same year she became the first Head of the Child Development Department of the Institute of Education, University of London, from where she was a great advocate of Nursery schooling. She corresponded with Piaget but the two never met.

Susan Isaacs was a powerful mix of 'educationalist' and 'psychologist' and at the centre of her child-centred philosophy was the need to understand the child from within. She argued that young children need a subtle balance between explorative freedom and emotional expression, and the need for mild, yet firm, supporting control in order to protect them from their inner anxieties and aggressive impulses.

Key texts:

The Nursery Years (1929)
Intellectual Growth in Young Children (1930)
Social Development of Young Children (1933)

Quotations:

'The nursery school teacher no less than the mother must have love and sympathy, natural insight and the patience to learn; but children need more than this in their struggles with the many problems we have glimpsed. They need true scientific understanding as well as mother-wit and mother-love.' (Isaacs 1954: 30)

'The nursery school is an extension of the function of the home, not a substitute for it; but experience has shown that it brings to the child such a great variety of the benefits that it can be looked upon as a normal institution in the social life of any civilised community.' (ibid.)

Biographies:

Gardner, D. E. M. (1969) *Susan Isaacs*. London: Routledge and Kegan Paul.

Louis Christian Schiller

Born: 20 September 1895, New Barnet

Died: 11 February 1976, Kenton, London

Personal details: Christian Schiller fought and was wounded in the First World War. In 1917 he was awarded the Military Cross, then studied maths at Cambridge (1919–20). He married Lyndall Handover in 1925 and had four children: three daughters and one son, Russell.

Profession(s):   Schiller taught maths in a secondary school until 1923. He took an interest in elementary and primary education and gained a teaching diploma in 1924. He became an Assistant Inspector in 1924 and District Inspector in Liverpool in 1925. Schiller ran HMI residential courses for serving teachers, often in collaboration with Robin Tanner who also promoted progressive education and the arts in primary education.

In 1946 he was appointed first Staff Inspector for Primary Education, following the 1944 Education Act.

Schiller became Senior Lecturer at the Institute of Education, University of London, and ran courses for teachers there between 1955 and 1963. He was a member of the Plowden Committee.

Key contributions to early childhood education: An HMI who promoted child-centred teaching, Schiller was a strong advocate for education and the arts in the early years. He influenced many teachers who went on to develop careers in teaching and promoting progressive methods.

Key texts: *Christian Schiller in His Own Words*, ed. Christopher Griffin Beale, (1979)
Many lecture scripts are in the Institute of Education archives: http://www.ioe.ac.uk/library/archives/ta.html

Quotations: 'Curriculum is not an attractive word … it leaves an impression of something sharp … ' (Schiller 1950 in Griffin Beale 1979)

'Assessment must take place "in the round". To see her assessment in the round we must observe *how* she reads. With what quality of understanding.' (ibid.)

Lev Semenovich Vygotsky

Born: 1896, Orsha, Belarus

Died: 1934

Personal details: Born into a middle-class family, Vygotsky studied lit-
                     erature at the University of Moscow. As a secondary
                     teacher he became interested in the processes of
                     learning and of the role of language in learning. He
                     then pursued his interest in psychology, studying
                     Freud, Piaget and Montessori in particular.
                        Vygotsky died at the age of 38 of tuberculosis, curtail-
                     ing the contribution he might have made to the field.

Profession(s):   Psychologist and educational theorist.

Key contributions   Vygotsky put forward the idea of learning as a social
to early childhood exchange, that young children learn through inter-
education: action with other children and with adults.
                        The 'Zone of Proximal Development' was a key con-
                     tribution to present understanding of the role of the
                     adult (or another child) in children's learning and is a
                     cornerstone of present-day pedagogy, where children
                     work together in groups, and of teachers' use of obser-
                     vation to inform their practice in the early years.

Key texts: *Mind in Society: The Development of Higher Psychological
                        Processes* (1980)
                     Thought and Language (1986)

Quotations: 'Learning and development are interrelated from the
                     child's very first day of life.' (Vygotsky 1980)

                     '... development is subject to the influence of the
                     same two main factors which take part in the organic
                     development of the child, namely the biological and
                     the social.' (ibid.)

                     '... human learning presupposes a specific social nature
                     and a process by which children grow into the intellec-
                     tual life of those around them.' (Vygotsky 1980: 88)

Biographies: Newman, F. and Holzman, L. (1993) *Lev Vygotsky:
                        Revolutionary Scientist*. London: Routledge.

Donald Woods Winnicott

Born: 28 January 1896, Plymouth, Devon

Died: 1971, London

Personal details: Winnicott's family were wealthy Methodists. His father, Sir Frederick, was a merchant and his mother was Elizabeth Martha Woods. He grew up in Plymouth, completed a medical degree at Cambridge in 1920 and served, during his student years, as a probationary surgeon in the First World War. Winnicott was married to Alice Taylor in 1923 and later to psychoanalyst Elsie Clare Nimmo Britton in 1958.

Profession(s):   A paediatrician and psychoanalyst for children at Paddington Green Hospital for Children (1923–63).

Key contributions to early childhood education: Winnicott developed concepts such as the 'holding environment', and the 'transitional object' (often referred to as the comfort blanket). His work has helped many teachers and early childhood educators to understand the needs of stressed and distressed children and to support children at times of transition in their lives. Winnicott put forward the idea of the *good-enough mother*, a mother whose physical and emotional attunement to her baby helps her baby to adapt without trauma to changes, including eventual realisation on the part of the baby that he/she is separate from his/her mother.

He was author of some 50 publications on parent–child relationships, child psychoanalysis, transitional objects, play, disorders or behaviour.

Key texts: 'Transitional objects and transitional phenomena' (1953)
Mother and Child: A Primer of First Relationships (1957)
The Child, the Family and the Outside World (1964)
The Family and Individual Development (1965)
Playing and Reality (1971)
Deprivation and Delinquency (1984)
Human Nature (1988)
Talking to Parents (1993)
Thinking about Children (1996)

Quotations:

'The good-enough mother ... starts off with an almost complete adaptation to her infant's needs, and as time proceeds she adapts less and less completely, gradually, according to the infant's growing ability to deal with her failure.' (Winnicott 1953).

'I suggest that the mother hates the baby before the baby hates the mother, and before the baby can know his mother hates him.' (From 'Hate in the Transference', 1947)

'The potential space between baby and mother, between child and family, between individual and society or the world, depends on experience which leads to trust. It can be looked upon as sacred to the individual in that it is here that the individual experiences creative living.' (From 'The location of cultural experience', 1967)

Biographies:

Rodman, F. R. (2003) *Winnicott: Life and Work*. Cambridge, MA: Perseus Publishing.

Jean Piaget

Born: 9 August 1896, Neuchatel, Switzerland

Died: 16 September 1980, Geneva, Switzerland

Personal details: Jean Piaget was the oldest child of a professor of medieval literature. At the age of 11, while studying at the local Latin high school, Piaget wrote a short paper on an albino sparrow – the first paper that perhaps sparked a career which resulted in over 60 books.

Piaget was married to Valentine Châtenay in 1923 and had three children, Jacqueline, Lucienne and Laurent. Much of Piaget's theory of intellectual development in childhood was informed by his observations of his own children.

Profession(s):   Piaget trained as a zoologist who began studying psychology as a result of his interest in the connection between biology and logic. Professor of psychology at Geneva University, his work became mainly concerned with the cognitive stages of development in children. Such studies have had an influence on practices for teaching in schools, as Piaget believed that learners assimilate and accommodate new knowledge at times of 'conflict' with their existing understanding of the world.

Key contributions to early childhood education: Piaget's many experiments were concerned with observing and analysing egocentric behaviour in young children in the belief that overcoming such behaviour was the goal of development. He saw learning as a process, which evolves as the result of children interacting with the environment and moving through certain stages of cognitive development. He corresponded with Susan Isaacs, though the two never met. Bärbel Inhelder (1913–97) was Piaget's research companion for 50 years.

The Sensori-Motor Stage lasts from birth to 2 years, followed by the Preoperational Stage (2 to 7 years), the Concrete Operational Stage (7 to 12 years) and the Formal Operational Stage (12 to adult).

In more recent times some researchers have questioned the basis of some of Piaget's theories. Most notably, Margaret Donaldson in her book *Children's Minds* (1986) considered that Piaget's experiments were too abstract for children to really perform appropriately well in. The belief is that some of Piaget's conclusions about young children's cognitive abilities do not have enough credibility and therefore do not accurately reflect the intellectual accomplishments of which many very young children are capable.

Key texts:
'Jean Piaget (Autobiography)', in E. G. Boring (ed.), *A History of Psychology in Autobiography, Vol. 4* (1952)
The Psychology of the Child (1969), with Bärbel Inhelder – originally published 1966
The Child's Conception of the World (1929) Harcourt, Brace: New York.

Quotations:
'The teacher-organiser should know not only his own science but also be well versed in the details of the development of the child's or adolescent's mind.' (Piaget 1969)

'Intelligence organizes the world by organizing itself.' (Piaget 1969)

Biographies:
Gattico, E. (2001) *Jean Piaget*. Milan: Bruno Mondadori.
Kitchener, R. (1986) *Piaget's Theory of Knowledge*. New Haven, CT: Yale University Press.
Smith, L. (1996) *Critical Readings on Piaget*. London: Routledge.

Erik Erikson

Born: 15 June 1902, Frankfurt, Germany

Died: 12 May 1994, Harwich, Massachusetts

Personal details: Erikson's Danish father left Erikson's mother before his birth. His Jewish mother, Karla Abrahamsen, was a lone parent for the first three years of his life until she married Dr Theodor Homberger, and the family moved to southern Germany. The young Erik Homberger first learned of his Jewish roots as a young man, and was taunted in the synagogue school for being Danish and at grammar school for being Jewish. Perhaps this is the root of Erikson's professional interest in identity.

He taught art, studied for a certificate in Montessori education and another from the Vienna Psychoanalytic Society. He was married with three children, and some of his life was spent on the move to avoid Nazi occupation. He left Vienna, Copenhagen, and subsequently moved to Boston when the Nazis entered Austria. He worked at the Harvard Medical School and practised child psychoanalysis. He was attracted to the work of anthropologists of the time as well as that of psychoanalysts. He taught at Yale and the University of California at Berkeley and carried out studies of the relationship between society and culture. He became Erik Erikson on taking American citizenship.

From 1950, he spent ten years working and teaching in Massachusets, and returned to Harvard in 1960 where he worked until his retirement in 1970.

Profession(s):   Psychologist and psychotherapist.

Key contributions to early childhood education: Erikson embellished Freud's suggestion of five stages of development to eight, extending the theory into adulthood. He promoted the notion of interaction between generations – mutuality – and highlighted the impact that children have on their parents as well as vice versa.

Erikson believed that development took place in stages, and that identity and convictions become stronger with time and experience. He believed that the stages of development were determined by nature and the limits within which nurture operates. According to Erikson, everyone moves through every stage and healthy development and learning in each stage was crucial to progression. In Erikson's view, physical, emotional and psychological stages of development are linked to specific experiences. For example, if an infant's physical and emotional needs are met, the infant completes his/her task of developing the ability to trust others. Unmet needs make it harder, if not impossible, to complete the various 'tasks' associated with each stage. And even though they may progress developmentally to the next 'stage', they lack something in their development. For example, if an 18-month-old is not given opportunities to explore and learn through his/her actions, the result can be a toddler who harbours self-doubt, thus hindering the later development of independence.

His work supports the development of programmes in early childhood education which foster positive self-esteem and exploratory learning through play.

Key texts:	*Childhood and Society* (1950) *Young Man Luther: A Study in Psychoanalysis and History* (1958) *Youth: Change and Challenge* (1963) *Insight and Responsibility* (1964) *Identity: Youth and Crisis* (1968)
Quotations:	'Hope is both the earliest and the most indispensable virtue inherent in the state of being alive. If life is to be sustained hope must remain, even where confidence is wounded, trust impaired.' (Erikson 1950) 'Babies control and bring up their families as much as they are controlled by them; in fact the family brings up the baby by being brought up by him.' (Erikson 1950) 'Healthy children will not fear life if their elders have integrity enough not to fear death.' (ibid.) 'Children love and want to be loved and they very much prefer the joy of accomplishment to the triumph

of hateful failure. Do not mistake a child for his symptom.' (Erikson 1963)

'Doubt is the brother of shame.' (ibid.)

Biographies:

Coles, R. (1970) *Erik H. Erikson: The Growth of His Work*. Boston, MA and Toronto: Little, Brown.

Friedman, L. J. (1999) *Identity's Architect: A Biography of Erik H. Erikson*. New York: Charles Scribner.

Miller, P. (1983) *Theories of Developmental Psychology*. San Francisco, CA: W. H. Freeman and Company.

Roazen, P. (1976) *Erik H. Erikson: The Power and Limits of a Vision*. New York: The Free Press.

Santrock, J. (1996). *Child Development*. Dubuque, IA: Brown and Benchmark Publishers.

Welchman, K. (2000) *Erik Erikson, His Life, Work, and Significance*. Philadelphia, PA: Open University Press.

Carl Rogers

Born:	8 January 1902, Oak Park, Illinois, Chicago
Died:	4 February 1987, San Diego, California

Personal details: Rogers' father was a civil engineer and his mother a devout Christian who brought her children up strictly; he was the fourth of six children. Aged 12, his family moved to a farm outside Chicago. He began to study agriculture at the University of Wisconsin but changed to study religion and then later doubted some of his basic religious views.

He married Helen Elliot and moved to New York, where he studied at the Union Theological Seminary but eventually rejected religion in favour of psychology. He gained a PhD in clinical psychology from Columbia University in 1931 after which he worked as a child psychologist and began to develop his own approach to therapy.

In 1942, he wrote *Counselling and Psychotherapy* and set up a counselling centre at the University of Chicago in 1945. In 1957, he returned to the University of Wisconsin, moving to La Jolla, California in 1964 to continue his research. He worked as a therapist and lectured and wrote until he died.

Profession(s): Psychologist and psychotherapist.

Key contributions to early childhood education: Rogers saw people as basically good or healthy and for him mental illness, criminality, and other such problems were not natural tendencies but arose because the person was not in a healthy state of mind. This theory was simple. He believed that human beings had in their nature to do the very best they can. The self-actualisation of the human being was the goal and all that a person did contributed to (or detracted from) the ability of that person to reach that goal. He is best known for his non-directive therapy.

His view of freedom and non-directive approaches have underpinned some thinking about how young children learn and how their needs in the early years might be best met in order to ensure positive mental health and growth. He advocated 'facilitating learning' through a genuine relationship between teacher and pupil. His work held notions of prizing, trusting and accepting the learner and of working through and with 'empathic understanding'. These concepts are central to many early childhood programmes which seek to adopt a holistic approach to learning and development. Key to Rogerian approaches were the relationships on which learning were based and through which learning took place and how person-centred learning can be used in education settings.

Key texts: *On Becoming a Person: A Therapist's View of Psychotherapy* (1961)
Freedom to Learn (1969), with H. J. Freiberg
A Way of Being (1980)

Quotations: 'When I look at the world I'm pessimistic, but when I look at people I am optimistic.' (Rogers 1961)

'The only person who is educated is the one who has learned how to learn and change.' (ibid.)

'In my early professional years I was asking the question: How can I treat, or cure, or change this person? Now I would phrase the question in this way: How can I provide a relationship which this person may use for his own personal growth?' (Rogers 1969)

'The good life is a process, not a state of being. It is a direction not a destination.' (Rogers 1980)

Biographies: Cohen, D. (1997) *Carl Rogers: A Critical Biography*. London: Constable.
Kirschenbaum, H. (1979) *On Becoming Carl Rogers*. New York: Delacorte Press.
Thorne, B. (1992) *Carl Rogers*. London: Sage.

Burrhus Frederic (B. F.) Skinner

Born: 20 March 1904, Susquehanna, Pennsylvania

Died: 18 August 1990, Cambridge, Massachusetts

Personal details: Skinner's father was a successful lawyer and his mother a housewife. He had one younger brother. He studied at Hamilton college, then worked in a bookshop where he read the work of psychologists Pavlov and Watson. He gained a PhD in psychology at Harvard University in 1931. In 1936, aged 32, Skinner was married with two daughters. He then became a teacher. During the Second World War he was funded to work on a secret project to train pigeons to keep pecking a target that would hold a missile onto a target. Later in his life he focused on moral and philosophical implications of behaviourism, completing his last paper the day he died.

Profession(s): In 1945 he became Chair of the psychology department at the University of Indiana. He returned to Harvard in 1948 and became Edgar Pierce Professor of psychology there in 1958.

Key contributions to early childhood education: Skinner developed and promoted a controversial philosophy of 'radical' behaviourism which involved (re)training people using a stimulus response technique, known as 'operant conditioning'. His ideas have been applied to programmes for bringing up children, training animals and classroom control. Skinner developed teaching machines based on the idea of programmed instruction where, through careful sequencing, students responded to material broken into small steps. Some of these ideas, particularly the breaking of behaviour into small learning steps, have been used, not always without controversy, in work with children with autism.

Key texts: *The Behavior of Organisms: An Experimental Analysis*
                     (1938)
                     Science and Human Behavior (1953)
                     Beyond Freedom and Dignity (1972)
                     About Behaviorism (1974)
                     Walden Two (1976)

Quotations: 'Behaviourism removes us from the pedestal of
                     god-like, and it places us with our ancestors, the
                     animals.' (Skinner 1938)

                     'Man is a complex chicken.' (ibid.)

                     'The hypothesis that man is not free is essential to
                     the application of scientific method to the study of
                     human behaviour.' (Skinner 1953)

                     'The consequences of behaviour determine the prob-
                     ability that the behaviour will occur again.' (Skinner
                     1974)

Biographies: Skinner, B. F. (1976) *Particulars of My Life*. New York:
                     Alfred A. Knopf.
                     See also the B. F. Skinner Foundation: http://www.
                     bfskinner.org/index.asp

Robin Tanner

Born:	1904, Bristol
Died:	1988, Wiltshire
Personal details:	Married Heather Sprackman in 1931.
Profession(s):	Artist, etcher, printmaker and HMI. From 1924, after attending Goldsmith's College, Tanner taught in Greenwich, Corsham and Chippenham. He was an HMI of primary schools from 1935 to 1964 and promoted the teaching of fine art to young children. As an HMI he ran courses for primary teachers, often with Christian Schiller.
Key contributions to early childhood education:	Tanner believed that it was essential for teachers and children to study natural things and that the arts and crafts, music and poetry should be central to primary education. He worked with Schiller on professional development courses for teachers.
Key texts:	Tanner wrote a number of books on printmaking aimed at children, including *Wiltshire Village* which was reprinted in 1978. His papers are held at the Institute of Education of the University of London, archives: http://www.ioe.ac.uk/library/archives/ta.html
Quotations:	'We know we are right and we are unassailable! But because we want all children to grow their roots deep into the finest strata of the civilisation of which they are a part, we need to be constantly vigilant and alert to possible inroads. And if we need any reward for our devotion it is surely to see children finding themselves, and learning and growing to their full structure.' (Tanner 1977)
Biographies:	Roscoe, B. (1990) 'Robin Tanner and the Crafts Study Centre', in B. Roscoe (ed.), *Tributes to Robin Tanner 1904–1988*. Bath: Holburne Museum and Crafts Study Centre.

3 Talking of Early Childhood Education: Six 'Conversations'

This part of the book brings together the ideas and practices of those whose biographies were presented in Part 2. They are, as it were, 'brought to life' in a series of imagined exchanges between some of those characters in conversation.

In this way a range of issues which lie at the very heart of the development and practice of early childhood education and care in the present day is explored by reaching back into history and relating past happenings and perspectives to present concerns and contexts. Throughout these conversations we highlight familiar themes: curriculum and pedagogy; ideologies of childhood; play; literacy; the role of the adult; the roles of parents; social and economic deprivation. While the conversations focus on a small number of historical figures, many others are referred to as their influence is discussed.

But before we begin to imagine how figures from history might have talked with us, we have included a conversation which took place between the three of us, and indeed, gave birth to the book in this form. A fairly casual exploration of the question, 'Do we need history?' (in early childhood education) led us to a focus on the part history has played in each of our careers and how it has informed our interests in early childhood. This conversation is then followed by four imaginary conversations which address different themes through the perspectives and work of different historical figures. The sixth, and final conversation is again in real time and explores some influence of history on current concerns.

Some thoughts of Albert Einstein …

The distinction between past, present and future is only a stubbornly persistent illusion.

The important thing is not to stop questioning. Curiosity has its own reason for existing. One cannot help but be in awe when he contemplates the mysteries of eternity, life, of the marvellous structure of reality. It is enough if one tries merely to comprehend a little of this mystery every day.

Never lose a holy curiosity.

Teaching should be such that what is offered is perceived as a valuable gift and not as a hard duty.

Albert Einstein 1879-1955

Conversation 1

So, who needs history?

In conversation:
Peter Clough (PC), **Cathy Nutbrown** (CN) and **Philip Selbie** (PS)

It is 1.30 p.m. on a winter afternoon in Prague, 19 November 2006, and three people meet in the Café Louvre looking out over snow-covered streets, drinking tea and talking about their project on the history of early childhood education. Founded in 1902, the Café Louvre has been host to many gatherings of hearts and minds, Kafka, his friends, artists, and Albert Einstein. It was usual in this place to linger for hours, and around the three, others meet and talk, read, conduct their business … People come and go and the three, absorbed in their own concerns, talk on …

In this conversation **Peter Clough**, **Cathy Nutbrown** and **Philip Selbie** are talking about what is important to them in early childhood education and why history matters …

PS   I think what I'd really like is a revolution … No, really! I'd like to picture us three here as revolutionaries, so many have plotted here, kicked against oppressive regimes … I have a sort of imagining that we could follow in the footsteps of those who also opposed the establishment … we could declare: 'In the name of freedom from the shackles of "Whitehall know-alls" we do hereby declare the foundation of a new state of affairs. One in which individuals can be individuals and the rights of children to learn as children will be safeguarded from the excessive intrusion of the state …'

CN   Radical!

PS   No, but I mean it … what's been going on and why are we letting young children become more and more oppressed by the dictats of government? Why isn't anybody listening to the stuff that has been spoken of for years ... decades ... about how children learn and what they need for optimim learning and what's important in the early years ...?

CN   Robin Tanner writes of how Christian Schiller wanted a revolution, 'a quiet and bloodless one, demanding a change of heart from teachers, and an emphasis on observation, self-appraisal, resilience and total dedication.'[1] I think that's the kind of revolution you're talking about ...

PS   There were lots of 'revolutionaries' in that sense ... Pestalozzi talked of the importance of children learning through their senses, discovering meaning for themselves; Comenius talked of children as seeds to be nurtured and teachers as 'gardeners'; Susan Isaacs showed how close observation of children in a rich environment of discovery ...

CN   And knowledgeable teachers ...

PS   ... how those things bring about rich learning. So where's all that gone? What's happened ...?

CN   We don't teach beginning early years practitioners their history anymore. In their initial training they don't get the riches from Comenius, or Pestalozzi, or Charlotte Mason; they may get a bit of Isaacs, Piaget ... but ... well ... that's why I think Masters' level students need to engage with those things, rediscover, or visit anew, those works.

PC   'Insanity is doing the same thing over and over again and expecting different results' – Einstein, I think ...

CN   Not learning from history is a kind of insanity ... Especially not learning what works ... what's effective and what is a total disaster ... and great ideas from the past have to be 'dug out' and dusted off and we have to be reminded, for example, that in the 1800s Charlotte Mason promoted parents, well mothers ... as key educators of their young children and the home as an environment for learning. I remember asking someone from the DfES why the Early Years Foundation Stage[2] did not acknowledge any previous work, because it had no grounding, not a single reference to any earlier work. She said that politicians have to think that things are their own ideas and so talking about the past, about something that has already been done, isn't likely to be a popular idea with them. Telling them 'But we knew this in the sixteenth century' doesn't cut much ice ... it seems politicians are the original re-inventors of wheels!

PC   But some policies have made a difference, surely ...

CN   I think there have been initiatives over the centuries which have made a difference, not all driven by government. In fact sometimes governments

---

[1] Robin Tanner, 'The way we have come'. Lecture to the Plowden Conference, date (Lincoln: Bishop Grosseteste College, 1977), p. 8.

[2] QCA (Qualifications and Curriculum Authority)/DfEE (Department for Education and Employment), *Curriculum Guidance for the Foundation Stage* (London: QCA/DfEE, 2000).

have been pushed, shamed even, into doing something because initiatives by religious groups and some individuals have been shown to be worth while. Some by wealthy businessmen such as Robert Owen, but also Steiner in partnership with Emil Molt, and then relatively 'lone' women – Maria Montessori, Rachel and Margaret McMillan, Charlotte Mason – doing hugely important work with young children to provide education for young children which is meaningful, respectful, fitting for their needs and also working to counterbalance the awfulnesses of life which some young children and their families face. And there's Sure Start in the UK, of course, massive investment and according to evaluations – yes – it's made a difference. Some policies have made a difference to combating poverty, through early intervention.

PC   I guess it must have done – surely? But I'm wary of a sort of Whig history of this – that things have gotten inexorably better – because despite the indicators (and Mr Blair's assurances) much has not changed for many children – in the UK, let alone in developing countries ... The poverty has been re-defined and re-distributed, but it's as acute as ever for those in its grip and – as they say – the gap between rich and poor gets bigger ...

CN   True ... and then funding stops and a new prime minister with a new government seeks to make his own 'new' mark ...

PS   I'm inclined to agree with Peter here! In theory, investment of one sort or another (time, energy, money, expertise, etc.) must contribute towards the fight against poverty for the very young. In practice though, I think the results are likely to be disproportionately small compared to the massive input. This is a wild 'gut feeling' response based on little hard evidence, but on a world-wide scale the size of the problem is really huge isn't it? I am not sure anyone is capable of measuring it accurately enough to confidently say 'this or that initiative has made a positive difference'. That does not discount the tremendous work that individuals or organisations do in this area and the clearly visible changes that have taken place for some children. I'm not advocating giving up trying to make things better either!

CN   But I really do think Sure Start made a difference – at least one independent study shows that[3] – but is it the 'tip of the iceberg'? And it's the perpetual fight for funding that's the big difficulty and new initiative after new initiative ... But the McMillans knew about bringing together the expertise of health and education; multi-disciplinary approaches to early years provision isn't new – just needed a policy direction and funding. The likely success of Sure Start as a concept was there in the history books. That's why history is important ...

PC   But I think you have to be old enough to really get a sense of how history helps ... I think you develop an interest in history as you accumulate more

---

[3] J. Weinberger, C. Pickstone and P. Hannon (eds), *Learning from Sure Start: Working with Young Children and their Families* (Buckingham: Open University Press, 2005).

of your own – I mean I don't think it interested me when I was younger … but I can now see how my own history – my own biography – was shaped by the times I was born and brought up in, and how as a person and a teacher I inherited a world of meanings laid down by other people and their values and their times. And that helps me to contest them, to take issue with some of the things we do now simply because they're hallowed by past traditions and legislation … I'll tell you a good example of that – IQ testing. When you understand the social and economic and political conditions that gave rise to that – and some of the social engineering as well as downright corrupt research practices that were involved – you can start to see how that way of thinking infected our whole approach to what children can and can't do, and how decisions were made that closed so many doors for so many children. All right, things have changed, but that 'innate ability' idea still infects a lot of what we do, a lot of our attitudes to children … So we're all part of a weave of ideas, and I think it's important to understand some of the other threads – the less visible ones – that give us the fabric of practice that we're part of. And of course, there are lots of good threads in there as well – that's why we want, in this book, to expose some of the weave, so we can all give a good account of what we do and why we're doing it, and why we might want to change it …

PS   I find looking at what other people have achieved in the past a great inspiration for me. I get all motivated especially when I read about people like Robert Owen who had a vision for making life better for people, especially when the motives are altruistic. Sure, there have been mistakes made in the past although some of those are only considered so with the benefit of hindsight. That in itself is not a bad thing as the clarity of insight that comes with the passing of time is refreshing, sometimes even breathtaking. I certainly want to discover what is the best I can do for young children in the time in which I have to make an impact. I think the best way to do that is to base at least some of my aspirations for the future on understanding what has happened in the past.

CN   But how can you avoid the bad stuff? When politicians make you do things … Take Baseline Assessment for example, it was wrong … should never have happened … bad for children, parents, teachers … yet everyone had to do it because it was a legal requirement … Past knowledge told us that and yet it still happened … A whole generation of children and teachers went through that … The beginning of a prescribed curriculum for under fives (even though they said it wasn't), Desirable Outcomes (1989) quickly followed by Baseline Assessment … Ofsted inspections. The loss of early years advisers who seemed to become 'Inspectors' overnight; the loss of the true HMI – of the Schiller kind – and the creation of a new breed of inspectors who were seemingly 'enemies' of the profession. But I think that the 1990s saw a real recognition of early years – suddenly all the campaigning and lobbying came to something, and the early years were attracting funding, being taken seriously, and seen to be a means of addressing some of the difficulties of poverty, ill-health, and those 'cycles' of deprivation. But of course with the additional funding and recognition came the 'strings' – funding came at a price – and there were conditions. One of them was that teachers should stop thinking for themselves and do as the new glossy documents told them … And a whole generation of early years professionals were de-skilled. I couldn't believe it recently when a group of teachers asked me if I would help them think about ways of observing children for assessment – they'd never done it, never been taught to do it, never been permitted to ask insightful questions of their own practice …

PS   Politicians, no doubt about it, have had a negative impact, but Cathy is point-ing to positives here as well, in terms of recognition and funding. But I think that as soon as education becomes linked to government policy then the rot sets in.

PC   You can't have a state education system that's not linked to government policy!

PS   No … but what I mean is … At the very best they are well meaning but too easily misled; at the worst they have a deliberately manipulative educational agenda. The issue at stake really, though, is the adult's wish to systematise a child's world by producing procedures – guidelines – and programmes – curricula – in the misguided belief that all children are the same and need organising. Nonsense. Pure nonsense.

CN   Well not all countries have been so prescriptive with their under fives educa-tion. In Denmark – a state-subsidised system for kindergartens – their cur-riculum is 12 pages long … But think about it … what's really important? What, who, has influenced us and our thinking …?

PS   I have to say that when I first read about the life and work of Comenius I then really began to 'think' about learning in the early years. His blending of the material world of children with the spiritual realm fascinated me and from then on I became interested in seeking the answers to questions like 'why' and 'how best to' in the context of education. Also, when I was training to be a teacher, the work of Matthew Lipman in the US made me realise that young children were capable of quite complex philosophical discussions. The *Socrates for Six Year Olds* film[4] made me realise that as a teacher I should never count on the fact that wisdom was necessarily the product of age!

CN   So you were compelled by the ideas of others, carefully thinking about what young children really could do …

PC   They're mainly 'local' people for me – your own work Cathy, and Peter Hannon's – working in the same department for many years helped me realise what I'd been missing! But a particular teacher – Joyce Rushton – I worked near, years ago, brought it home – a relentless commitment to overcoming difficulties, mostly made by institutional systems, maximising achievements, championing individuals, detecting crap and standing up to ignorant bullies in systems … Of writers/researchers, I think Tony Booth and Margaret Donaldson opened my

---

[4] http://sapere.org.uk

windows – letting in the light on the darknesses that surround our educational practices ...

CN See, it's people and their ideas for all of us! For me, there are three people from my days as a young teacher, two I worked with – Ann Hedley and Ann Sharp – they taught me so much about how young children learn, and the role of their families and of how to make provision 'fit' children's learning. Ann Hedley taught me about working with parents, about working respectfully with other human beings whatever their role or their age. Ann Sharp taught me about children's play – about how to create exciting opportunities for play, outdoors as well as indoors. And the third person is Chris Athey – her work on Schemas and children's thinking has stayed with me since the day I first heard her speak when I was a young teacher in Sheffield, and my first copy of her book is still full of pencil notes and Post-Its! Later, it was Peter Hannon who taught me the importance of research and real critical enquiry into what was effective in early childhood education. So it's those ideas, and the models others have given us ...

PS And I bet it's the same for books ... If you had to choose, which book would you take to your desert island?

CN Ah – the works of Susan Isaacs I think – so that I could read again and continue to think about those rich observations of play which she made at the Malting House, yes, and even though she was working in a situation where poverty and difficulty were not to the fore, what's there in her observations is uninterrupted play when conditions are at their best. Optimum conditions ... What you get with Isaacs' work is play in optimum conditions. So I'd like to take Isaacs' work with me. If I didn't get rescued, I'd do what I've been thinking of doing for years and that's to analyse them in terms of Schemas – it's all there ...

PC I think I'd take a complete works of Charles Dickens! It's all there – still: the pathos, the terror, the joy ... For a large majority of the world's children it's still to be found there ...

CN Mmmm ... well, I'd have to have *Great Expectations* – poor Pip being sent to 'play' for Miss Haversham's entertainment ... And then, which piece of children's fiction would I take ... *The Velveteen Rabbit*?[5] Becoming Real – I can still remember some of it by heart:

> *"What is REAL?" asked the Rabbit one day, "Does it mean having things that buzz inside you and a stick-out handle?"*
> *"Real isn't how you are made," said the Skin Horse. "It's a thing that happens to you. When a child loves you for a long, long time, not just to play with, but REALLY loves you, then you become Real."*
> *"Does it hurt?" asked the Rabbit.*

---

[5] Charles Dickens, *Great Expectations* [1861] (Harmondsworth: Penguin, 1994); Margery Williams, *The Velveteen Rabbit: Or How Toys Become Real* (New York: Avon Books, 1922).

> "Sometimes," said the Skin Horse.
>
> "Does it happen all at once, or bit by bit?" asked Rabbit.
>
> "It doesn't happen all at once," said the Skin Horse. "You become. It takes a long time. By the time you are Real, most of your hair has been loved off, and your eyes drop out and you get loose in the joints and very shabby. But these things don't matter at all, because once you are Real you can't be ugly, except to people who don't understand."

And I'd have to take *Guess How Much I Love You* – I know this too …

> 'Big Nutbrown Hare settled Little Nutbrown Hare into his bed of leaves. He leaned over and kissed him good night. Then he lay down close by and whispered with a smile, "I love you right up to the moon – AND BACK."'[6]

But that's also supposing that I still got the Bible and the complete works of Shakespeare. What about you Philip?

PS   I like the 'Nutbrown' connection …! Well, in the children's fiction for me, it would have to have copies of *The Whales' Song*[7] and *Nothing*[8] as, like the *Velveteen Rabbit*, they hold important messages about being human and the nature of being loved. I would also want a copy of *Children's Minds* by Margaret Donaldson as I think I could read that over and over again and still keep learning from it.[9] Then just to keep everything in perspective I would take *How Children Fail* by John Holt and *All I Really Need to Know I Learned in Kindergarten* by Robert Fulghum.[10]

CN   Yes – Robert Fulghum is a reminder of the political importance of early years curriculum and pedagogy …? Put things back where you found them … Clean up your own mess.

PC   In our book the focus is mainly on researchers/thinkers/practical 'doers' ostensibly concerned with early years as a research or policy topic, but there's a world of writers – writers of fiction as well as journalism – who have had more subtle but often equally penetrating insights into the early years … If I were designing my ideal early years programme for practitioners, I'd have an absolutely core component on … fiction and children's literature. And everybody should be made to memorise Wordsworth's *Prelude*!

CN   *There are in our existence spots of time,*
       Which with distinct pre-eminence retain
       A renovating Virtue, whence,
       … our minds …

---

[6] Sam McBratney, *Guess How Much I Love You* (London: Walker Books, 1994).

[7] Dyan Sheldon and Gary Blythe, *The Whales' Song* (London: Red Fox, 1993).

[8] Mick Inkpen, *Nothing* (London: Hodder and Stoughton, 1996).

[9] Margaret Donaldson, *Children's Minds* (London: Fontana, 1986).

[10] John Holt, *How Children Fail* (Hardmondsworth: Penquin, 1990); Robert Fulghum, *All I Really Need to Know I Learned in Kindergarten: Uncommon Thoughts on Common Things* (New York: Ivy Books, 1989).

PC *... Are nourished and invisibly repaired.*[11]

PS I know what you mean Peter. I think there should be an element in every teacher training programme and especially in early years, that makes people think 'outside the box' so to speak. Wordsworth's recollections of early childhood in his 'Ode: On Intimations of Immortality' might be food for thought in this respect. In it he suggests that for him as a young child 'There was a time when meadow, grove, and stream, the earth and every common sight, to [him] ... seem[ed] apparelled in celestial light'. He then makes it clear that this wonder at the world that is so characteristic of his early childhood has faded with age and 'The things which I have seen I now can see no more'.[12]

By the way, I also think that everyone should build a sandcastle on their birthday ...!

CN Say more about that ....

PS Well, to me there is something very special about watching young children playing with sand and water. They find endless possibilities to use it to develop their imagination and enter a world of their own as well as investigating its physical properties as a building material. I think as adults we would benefit in so many ways if every now and then we just messed about with something simple like sand and experimented with what we could do with it.

PC You mean try to be a child again?

PS Sort of! I mean it's not possible in one sense but good early years teaching is often seen when adults are interacting with children 'as one of them', for example around a water tray or in a role-play area. If as adults we took ourselves away to a simple sandpit somewhere and left behind some of today's 'sophisticated' classroom gadgets (dare I say interactive whiteboards ...), we might find out a lot about ourselves, let alone the children we teach.

CN That takes us back to the desert island Philip! I can see you would be happy to spend more time splashing in the water and digging in the sand rather than reading those 'essential texts' we talked about earlier ... But how did we get here? I mean what was it that actually brought us to early years and to it mattering so ... to it being so central to our professional lives?

PC Well, as you both know, I came late to early years – if you know what I mean! I started working life as an English and Drama teacher in secondary schools, but was always drawn to what was going wrong for kids – or more accurately what schools were doing to fail them – I was drawn to the pupils themselves as learners, rather than to teaching a 'subject'. I then worked in a number of

---

[11] William Wordsworth, *The Predule* [1805], Book XI, 1: 258–78, in William Wordsworth, *The Complete Poetical Works*, with an introduction by John Morley (London: Macmillan and Co., 1888).

[12] Wordsworth, 'Ode: On Intimations of Immortality', in *The Complete Poetical Works*.

Special Schools before moving to higher education, and I think it's only through working through countless studies that the realisation dawned that those early years are crucial – obvious, I know! – and that that is where exclusion and failure start …

PS   I didn't begin my career as a teacher, I decided to enter teaching in my late twenties after a relatively short career in the business world. I chose to train to teach 'infants' because for me I could see that was where the most 'fun' was to be found. I felt it would sort of fit with my personality as I enjoyed drawing, painting and especially making things as a child myself, and before my training I often found myself talking with young children and watching their sense of adventure and discovery when being creative. When I chose to work with early years children I think I felt I would discover more about the roots of this drive to learn and create. But Cathy, I bet you were always going to be a teacher! …

CN   Right! I was always going to be a teacher, it's sort of what girls did! I quickly became fascinated by children's thinking and I think it's true to say that 'watching them learn' was more interesting to me than thinking 'what shall I teach them next?'! I learned early on that following children's thinking was the best way for me to try to teach them. So the motivation for much of my work remains a deep curiosity (and awe) about how young children learn …

PS   What is it that we must say, in this book? What is it that we absolutely can't leave out?

PC   Well, we have to be able to justify our practices and a way of doing that is to stand on the shoulders of others. But life history, our own personal connections with our own pasts, is important too: people in our own lives, your gran, Mrs Yates, the teacher who took you on nature walks instead of making everyone draw flowers that all looked the same. And what we can do with our own life histories is to connect them with the lives and work of others from the past … It is less a question of counting up quotations – Pestalozzi said this or Piaget said that – so that you can trot them out … but of puzzling over them, disagreeing if you possibly can, and asking 'How does this fit with what *I* know of the world?' … and so arriving at a true philosophy of early years education *for myself* … a justification of *my* beliefs and practices. And I believe you do this by bringing together insights certainly from the Mighty Giants of educational history, but – no less importantly – lessons from your own family and schooling history, and some head-aching thinking about what you hold true and dear …

CN   … so that you can say: these are *my* colours, this is what I believe, this is my set of working principles, values, understandings … and these are the colours I want to nail to this mast. This is what I stand for, seek to do in my work … and it's because of these experiences, and that work, and that book and that child …

PC   … exactly that! Bringing together personal life experiences with the ideas, work, writings of others …

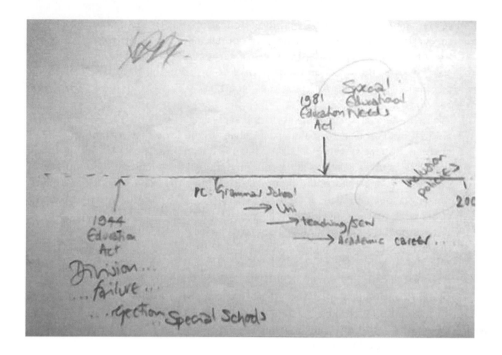

PS OK, so if we were each to map out the key points, events, people that had an impact on our lives, and the key players (for us) across this particular early childhood history, what would our maps look like?

[Peter starts to sketch out a sort of timeline.]

PC Well for me it would be ... these policy beginnings – and I can represent them literally like a timeline – a bit boring perhaps but it's true ... Policy really made a difference to the education/career paths I took. The 1944 Education Act gave rise to division ... failure ... rejection and the creation of Special Schools. For me, it heralded what I might call 'success' – grammar school education leading to a teaching and then university career. And then more highly significant policies, the 1981 Education Act and the creation of Special Educational Needs and then the inclusion policies of the 2000s ... all these have, in one way or another, formed part of the twists and turns of the current in which I have swum ...

CN That's really interesting – how you can trace the clear impact of policy on your own life and your professional career. And alongside that I want to put people – individuals. I'm struck by how almost everyone who inspires me from history – people who I think really DID something – were all doing

something else first. Early childhood education wasn't their first or primary
career. Well, that's obvious I guess, of course it wasn't, but they were all pursuing a different path, different sorts of careers and sort of 'came upon' early
childhood education – or realised that doing something for or with young
children was a way of pursuing their goals.

PS   Say more ... who ...?

CN   Well – Pestalozzi, seeing education and schooling as part of what we could call
a social intervention to make a difference to the lives of poor and orphaned
children. Robert Owen – a businessman – but with a particular set of social,
political – and yes religious and economic values, which led him to identify education for young children as important in building the New Lanark community.
Reading about all that is incredible – parenting classes, adult learning classes,
cooking, all sorts ... the original Sure Start!

PS   But you said they were all doing something else – who else?

CN   Maria Montessori – a medical doctor; Susan Isaacs – a psychoanalyst; Rachel
and Margaret McMillan – Christian Socialists ... one a medical doctor. Even
Florence Nightingale wrote letters about how young children should be educated. And 'ordinary' – though that's not the right term – working mothers,
desperate for something for their children, places to play.

PC   So what's key for you Cathy – what are you getting at when you say they were
all doing something else first ... Why is that important?

CN   I mean that history tells us – well tells me – that many people have, over the
centuries, looked to the development of early years provision as a way of
addressing (at least partially) social difficulties; nurseries during the war years
to cater for working mothers who were needed in the ammunition factories –
and in the process trying to provide healthy conditions (food, sleep, fresh
air for the children of the inner-city slums). That's one example ...
and take the formation of the Preschool Playgroups Association [PPA] in
the 1960s – founded because one working mother, Belle Tutaev, wrote a letter to the *Manchester Guardian* in 1961 saying something like 'are there any
other mothers out there who want somewhere for their young children to
play and learn together?' – and the campaign for nursery education. The
PPA was born and today the Pre-school Learning Alliance as it now is probably caters for provision for around 50 per cent of three- to five-year-olds
in Britain. But one woman lit the flame – that's the point. There were the
mothers of post-war, post-occupation Reggio Emilia, who worked together
to build a better future for the next generations – the beginning of the now
world-renowned Reggio Emilia Preschools and Toddler Centres; I've already
talked about Robert Owen. So what I'm saying is, there is nothing new
about people looking to early childhood education to change the world –
make it a better place. What's recent, in England, is government recognising
the role that early childhood education can play and putting some funding
into it.

PC   Enough funding?

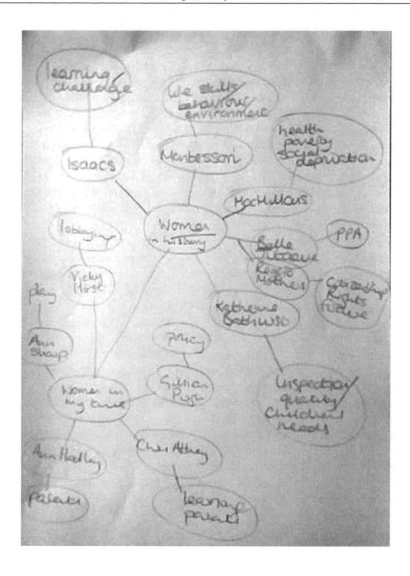

CN Well no, not enough, but more than ever before. At least politicians now realise that life begins before children are five years old! ... But that's where I'm coming from – it's what speaks to me. But I think you're right, Peter, in saying that the first step in thinking about early childhood education history is our own life/learning history and *then* making connections with the life, learning, work achievements of others ...

PS So Cathy – what's this you're scribbling ...?

CN Well I was just thinking about the roles of women in early childhood education and thinking who they were in my own early childhood education

career ... And I've got two groups really: those from history – and their contributions and what I take from them – and those I have known or still know
and their impact on me personally in my life and work ... But I think this is
limiting me – I don't want to confine myself to this recent history and the contribution of women because I *do* think that this would only be a partial history. Reggio Emilia, for example, owes much to those mothers of 1945 and
after but it wouldn't be what it is today without the work and commitment
and vision of Loris Malaguzzi. But there are some, how shall I put it, 'forgotten
women': Elizabeth von Grunelius, for example, who wrote and founded the
Steiner Kindergartens.[13] After Steiner's death, few outside the Steiner
Fellowship would know or talk of her – yet her contribution was huge.
Charlotte Mason – few people talk of her nowadays, and look at her work on
the outdoors, home learning, children's rights, teacher education ... And all
those mothers, grandmothers, older sisters – for generations and generations
bringing up young children – but yes – I wouldn't want to confine my thoughts
to women only ... brothers, fathers, grandfathers too – informal family care
and learning. And in my own work, Peter Hannon, for example, is a very important part of my own thinking and research career in terms of early literacy, and
the need to ask critical questions, so it's not helpful for me to only think of
women ... And Philip wouldn't be able to write his history of early education
without Comenius ... lots of men made a real difference ...

PS   Absolutely right! For me Comenius was a 'giant' not only in his vision for
reforming education but many aspects of society and politics too. He dreamed
of making the world a better place and wrote, lectured and travelled exten-
sively in his quest to do so and he did this against tremendous odds in his personal life at a time when Europe was involved in a terrible war. As I said earlier
I get inspired by people not only of vision but also of action in pursuit of
improving the quality of life not only for school children but also for humankind
generally. So, like Cathy, certain people who have sought to make a difference
have inspired me and helped form my historical perspective on my particular
professional outlook.

PC   Mmm ... You spent time in business before entering teaching. How did that
shape your perspective on what you do now?

PS   Well, I certainly felt that I could make more of a difference with my own life by
spending it with children rather than remaining in what I was doing in business
and that is why I decided to change careers when I did. However, I have not
been in a position to specifically use my experiences outside education to make
a difference like Maria Montessori or Susan Isaacs did.

CN   Didn't you once tell me that you began your training towards the end of the
1980s? Peter has talked about the influence of policy on his teaching career, so

---

[13] The Waldorf plan for early childhood education was published in Elizabeth von Grunelius,
Educating the Young Child (London: New Knowledge Books, 1955) and set out the underpinning
structures of Steiner-Waldorf Kindergarten provision.

did the legislation of that period have any influence on you as a student teacher?

PS   Yes, interestingly it did. We spent time studying the 1944 and the 1981 Education Acts that Peter mentioned, but my years as a student were spent coming to terms with the 1988 Education Act which introduced the National Curriculum and set the scene for all that was to follow. I remember being overwhelmed with subject folders and Attainment Targets and thinking what on earth had I done by deciding to become a teacher! However, having come from a business background there was part of me that initially found sympathy with some of the arguments put forward in defence of the massive changes that were beginning to have an impact on the profession. I particularly remember studying Jim Callaghan's Ruskin College speech of 1976 and thinking 'well, if people feel schools aren't producing the type of children that industry needs, then maybe something should be changed!'

PC   Oh, yes I forgot that one. That really was the beginning of recent government interference in mainstream education. It seems that everything has just been steamrollering on since then and children have been forgotten in the rush towards everything being almost 'sanitised'. You mentioned this at the beginning of our conversation when you said that there seemed to be an 'agenda' and adults were wishing to 'systematise a child's world'.

PS   Yes, I was not specifically training for early years then but certainly some of the controversial policy ideas that have happened recently have come as the principles surrounding the National Curriculum have been 'modified' to suit the care and education of very young children. With the benefit of hindsight it is clear to me that that children are not consistently at the centre of decisions made by policy-makers. By the time I completed my training and found myself teaching I had obviously changed my position from that of the ex-businessman! By the way, I have always felt a bit sorry for Jim Callaghan though, as I think his speech started something that ended up looking a lot different than he probably imagined it would!

CN   So, in a sense your influences, Philip, have been a mixture of people and policies ...

PS   I think in my case the two are rather less defined than Peter's and yours. Peter's timeline and your diagram are clearly visible on a piece of paper and show the development of your thinking. Maybe I can 'represent' my influences by taking you both back to that sandpit I mentioned earlier. Put the policies and the people in a bucket, give them a stir, turn them all upside down and then tap the bucket three times before lifting it up to see what is underneath. I am not sure if that is a useful image for you or not but it certainly fits with my childhood enjoyment in creating 'things' and I think in a sense that is what we do as teachers. We form ideas in our minds about how we are going to work with children and why we will do it a certain way, and then we try it out. Some of it is based upon experience, some on natural instinct and our own character but frankly some of it is pure experiment at times.

CN   So, policy, women, philanthropists, political lobbying, social justice, economics … it's all there in these histories, and it all adds up to the lives of men and women who wanted in some way to make a difference. They all saw young children as a future to be invested in and invested their intellect, energy and lives – as well as their money … So that's it – that's what this book is about: people's lives, people making a difference, people investing in children.

PS   Constructing a sound personal philosophy of early childhood education is built upon many different factors, perspectives and important historical influences. The thing to remember is that it doesn't really matter if your sandcastle falls over; what really matters is that you can always have another go at building one!

PC   Yes! And we have to remember that every day the tide will come in and wash away that sandcastle, so being able and willing to rebuild another day with different sand, maybe even on a different beach, is important. Things don't stay the same. Everything changes. And as Einstein said, 'Education is what remains after one has forgotten everything he learned in school …'

From the diary of Lady Margaret Smith[14]

A New Lanark imagining ...

It is 1817, late spring. I had arrived from London yesterday, having visited the opening of the exhibition of the Elgin Marbles at the British Museum, a fine display, and something which lifted the depression in this terrible post-war period. I stayed in Mr Owen's house last evening and, over dinner with him and other guests, we talked of his vision for society and consequently of his plans for education which would contribute to the development of such a society. He greeted me warmly as his guest and made it very clear that he did not hold the views of other eminent figures of the time that women should not be involved in social reform of educational progress. 'Women,' he said, 'Women will be no longer made the slaves of, or dependent upon men ... They will be equal in education, rights, privileges and personal liberty'.[15] When I read these very words some 20 or more years later, I was transported in my mind back to the dinner table and that spring evening in 1817. There was talk of the Typhus epidemic breaking out in Edinburgh and Glasgow and I recall my host discussing the opening of his 'Institute for the Formation of Character' when he said that a better society was one 'formed so as to exist without crime, without poverty, with health greatly improved, with little, if any misery, and with intelligence and happiness increased a hundredfold.' And I know he truly believed that only ignorance (at all levels) would prevent his vision from becoming a reality.

The first New Lanark school has been open for about a year and we visited the very next morning. Walking into the school yard I saw hordes of little children playing and a tall figure amongst them. He was a Mr James Buchanan, the first teacher in the New Lanark school, chosen by Mr Owen from his own workforce in the mills. I could see from his interactions with the children that he too holds dear Mr Owens' ideals of kindness, activity and co-operation. And, my first impression was that the importance of the outdoors, good wholesome food and space for rest was very apparent.

Some little children spotted Mr Owen and ran to him, enjoying his hand on their head, and smiling up as he spoke gentle words to them. Next, I was taken to the dancing room, where there were some 70 or more pairs of children, really very young, dancing with amazing accuracy to the piano music of the maypole celebrations. They smiled, sang, and danced with real joy.

There was good food available in a public kitchen, adult education classes, parent classes and support, community involvement, and health care. Truly there was something special at New Lanark which we should try to emulate throughout the Kingdom.

---

[14] Note: Lady Margaret Smith is a fictional character but the words of Owen and the events of the time are taken from real happenings.

[15] Robert Owen, *Book of the New Moral World: Sixth Part* [1841], 7 Parts (London, 1836–44), published as one volume (New York: G. Vale, 1845).

Conversation 2

Why early childhood education?

An imagined conversation between
John Comenius (JC) and **Robert Owen** (RO) with **Philip Selbie** (PS)

It is June 2007. Around the world there are many stories of poverty and neglect in childhood, and in the UK the British government has been pursuing an intervention policy designed to address some of the difficulties associated with poor beginnings in life. Sure Start, launched in 1998, has been in operation for some nine years – a multi-agency programme of provision which was designed to alleviate the difficulties associated with social disadvantage such as ill-health, unemployment, and underachievement.

In this imaginary conversation **Jan Amos Comenius** and **Robert Owen** are talking with **Philip Selbie** about why early education is important and how provision for young children is important to the development and well-being of wider society.

PS   Perhaps we should begin thinking about the purpose of early education by talking about childhood itself. You, Comenius, have lots to say about children and childhood … What, would you say, is your *philosophy* of childhood?

JC   We are right to begin by examining this important issue. Views about childhood form the very heart of my philosophy of education. In my opinion, children are precious gifts from God in whom He has planted His very image. Children from the youngest age deserve respect not only on account of whom they represent but also on account of who they will eventually become.

PS   I am interested that you choose the word 'respect'. How are you interpreting the word? Do you mean that respect for children implies an elevation of their status in society or that respect should be allowed to drift into some form of 'reverence' or 'indulgence'?

JC   No, not at all. What I am suggesting is that society at large, and adults in partic-ular, should afford children the time and space that is necessary for them to develop their full potential. In my opinion children, like all of us, are created in the image of God and so deserve to have their dignity respected. Also, children need protecting in the sense that they *are* vulnerable members of society. Children are valuable, delicate and beautiful or – to use an image from nature – they are like precious jewels and such things naturally inspire in all of us a respectful appreciation, almost, I would say, a ... 'reverence' on account of what they are by their very nature.

PS   Interesting – Nutbrown talks about 'respect' for children and childhood but I think she means something slightly different. Let me read this short extract to you and see what you think. She says that those who work with young children should respect all children, here ...

> *Not just those who are easy to work with, obliging, endearing, clean, pretty, artic-ulate, capable, but every child – respecting them for who they are, respecting their language, their culture, their history, their family, their abilities, their needs, their name, their ways and their very essence.*[16]

I think Nutbrown is thinking about this from the point of view of 'rights' and the United Nations Convention on the Rights of the Child from 1992, but you seem to be suggesting then that there is something inherent or latent in chil-dren that deserves our respect, almost in the same way that something may inspire a sense of awe or wonder.

JC   Yes, and that leads me to the fact that I also believe children deserve such respect because they hold within themselves enormous potential. They hold potential for themselves with regard to their own development but also – and I think this is important – potential for the development of those around them. This might include those they are in close relationship with, for example family and friends, but ultimately they hold potential for the development of society itself.

PS   That sounds like a heavy responsibility you are placing upon the shoulders of children!

JC   On the contrary, the burden of responsibility lies with those entrusted with the care and nourishment of children. Again, if I use an example from nature, there is huge potential in a seed to grow into a large tree with a strong, tall trunk, wide branches and, at the right time of the year, a full canopy of leaves. However, a seed will not grow to its fullest potential if it is not treated respect-fully and in the right manner.

PS   Are you saying, then, that the child – or to follow your analogy the seed – is to play no active part in discovering and realising its potential?

---

[16] Cathy Nutbrown, *Respectful Educators – Capable Learners: Children's Rights and Early Education* (London: Paul Chapman Publishing, 1996), p. 54.

JC No, I am not. Obviously, there is a greater and more visible portion of responsibility that falls to those of us entrusted with the upbringing of children.
However, I don't think that it follows that children are not responsible themselves for being co-agents of development too. Remember that I said earlier
that I was not advocating the indulgence of children but rather a healthy
respect for them.

PS Some would question your apparent idealism and argue that the very nature of
humankind is corrupt and sinful and this is clearly evident in young children. We
hear people talk of quite young children being manipulative, pushing adults so
that they get their own way. Some parents, especially those living in areas of
social disadvantage, are often so stressed by their children's behaviour that they
need medical as well as practical help. Young mothers may take anti-depressant
drugs; others need to attend support groups or family therapy. Children are
often considered in need of firm discipline administered by a strong authority
figure but some parents just can't do this. The profusion of television programmes about 'taming toddlers' and dealing with 'tiny tearaways' bears witness
to the difficulties some parents have. Some people today, as well as many in the
past, promote the opinion that children need to be controlled, sometimes as the
result of a conviction that is based in a particular theological point of view ... It
is interesting that you seem to be invoking certain religious language but without the customary zeal for character 'reformation'. Is this a fair interpretation
of your position?

JC Absolutely correct. I have no doubt about humankind's ability to perfect itself
given the time and the right conditions, although let me very quickly add two
essential qualifications to what I have just said. Firstly, I do not believe
humankind can do this alone. Every man, woman and child needs to work
towards this state of perfection reliant upon God and working in harmony
with Him. Such a journey, here on earth, is preparation for the next stage of
our development as created beings and continues on into eternity. As I have
written,

> As, then, it is certain that our sojourn in our mother's womb is a preparation for
> the life in the body, so certain is it that our sojourn in the body is a preparation
> for the life which shall follow this one, and shall endure forever.[17]

That's the best way I can express it. Secondly, while I do believe that people are
born with a susceptibility to sin and to be corrupted, I don't think that discipline is the complete 'answer' to this problem of human nature.

PS So is there a role for discipline in your model for human perfectibility?

---

[17] J. A. Comenius, *The Great Didactic of Jan Amos Comenius* [1657], translated into English and
edited with biographical, historical and critical introductions by M. W. Keatinge (London:
A. & C. Black, 1923), p. 34.

JC You may be surprised to hear me say this but, yes I do believe there is. However, not in the traditionally 'repressive' sense of the term that most people understand discipline to mean. I think that discipline is necessary and performs a 'corrective' role in childhood, but I would just prefer to interpret the word more broadly than most.

PS More broadly? What do you mean by that?

JC For instance, discipline should be present primarily in order to represent 'boundaries' for acceptable forms of behaviour not only for children but adults too. Also, I don't believe that forms of punishment should be administered in a violent or aggressive way. Such things run counterproductive to creating the ideal form of society that I believe is characterised by a peaceful and harmonious existence. Perhaps I should say at this point that I do not automatically endorse excessive freedom either. Such an alternative extreme only leads to chaos and disorder, which is equally counterproductive for children and society.

[For some while, Robert Owen has been listening intently, trying to find a suitable point at which to break in.]

RO Can I come in here? Now, I'm a businessman, but I think that industry has an important part to play in this business of education. In fact, industry can only really succeed if it is truly part of a community and its education system. I've tried to develop this in New Lanark. I really do think that the environment in which people live makes a difference to them as people. It's obvious really, but I feel a responsibility to my mill workers to do something about this. I believe that it's possible to nurture rational, good and humane people, but harsh treatment, by teachers, employers, whoever, can really corrupt people. Education is so important, that's why I built the school at New Lanark. When I arrived at New Lanark, children as young as five were working in the mills sometimes 12 or more hours a day – can you believe that? I decided right away not to employ children under ten and I saw to it that the young children went to the nursery and infant schools. I also banned any form of physical punishment in my schools and factories at New Lanark.

PS All right, so let me ask each of you how you see discipline making a significant contribution to childhood – how might children be disciplined in ways that shape them as human beings and help their learning?

JC May I respond first of all by returning to theological language? God created humankind to be 'master' of the created world and in my opinion that includes humankind itself. Men and women cannot hope to make progress for themselves or the lives of others if they are unable to master their own lives. I should make the point again here that such a form of discipline, or rather *self-discipline*, couldn't begin to be accomplished without the help of God.

PS You seem to lay great stress upon the importance of a healthy relationship with God as the basis for much of what you say.

JC I would go even further than that, and say that my philosophy generally is based upon the inseparable relationship of nature, man and God. It is not a popular way of looking at the world for many and indeed has been the reason for many fierce arguments, particularly in the development of thinking generally in seventeenth-century Europe.

PS And for a long time since! I would suggest that the same feeling still exists over 300 years later in twenty-first-century Europe. Incidentally, though there are people of faith – Christians, Muslims, Jews, Hindus, Buddhists, and others – there are also many moral and decent people who regard themselves as Humanist, Atheist, Agnostic. So I think we also need to respect the views of those who hold no clearly identifiable view of a 'higher authority' when forming a philosophy for education. Can I ask you, Robert Owen, for your perspective on discipline in early education? What is the philosophical basis for your position on punishment and discipline?

RO Cruelty by 'superiors' – teachers, employers, whoever – only ever ultimately results in badness – corruption in children's minds and people's hearts. On that basis I support a philosophy of education which does its best to reduce any need for punishment. Make people *want* to work, make children *want* to learn. Ensure workers are fit and well to work by providing housing, reward hard work with opportunities for recreation. Working seven days a week is bad and in the end would not be the best for my business – it's as simple as that. And reward children's efforts in school with times to play – indeed make them fit to learn by having them spend time outdoors, too.

PS So, you feel there is an economic case for this position you hold on punishment – in the end it's good for business as well as good morally …?

RO Yes, I think …

JC But we cannot do without God! Man ignores God and he perishes!

PS You both seem to take a similar and benevolent view of discipline and punishment, but your ideas seem to be born of different philosophies … Interesting … but let's go back to the earlier part of our conversation … You are both deeply committed to the education of young children, but can I ask both of you to say simply what you think is the purpose of education for young children?

JC Well, for me, first and foremost, I believe the purpose of education is to improve society and to make a major contribution to the reformation of all human affairs and that includes society, politics and the Church.

RO Couldn't really have put it better myself! I would want to add other things – the economy, and people as individuals – but essentially I agree.

PS Right … well, some people would disagree that the Church should have a central role now. Even though the Church of England and Quaker schools made an important early contribution to establishing schools, they have a different status now. Some people and politicians vehemently oppose 'faith' schools and others continue to argue that they play an essential role. But I think the idea of early education making a difference to society and politics of the country and to the economy as well as to individuals are ideas at the heart of the Sure Start policy which seeks to tackle deprivation. In this context of early intervention, I'd like to ask you two things: first, when do you think such early education should begin? And secondly, are there some children for whom early education is more beneficial than others?

JC   Mmmm ... complex questions, but I think even in this modern age where some have turned from God, I think education is a lifelong process. Education is a process which prepares the individual for eternity and so it begins from the moment of birth, or even earlier in some respects, and continues until death. Society should encourage lifelong learning and that should be the case for girls as well as boys in equal measure. As I have written:

> Nor can any sufficient reason be given why the weaker sex ... should be excluded from the pursuit of knowledge ... They are also formed in the image of God, and share in His grace and kingdom of the world to come.[18]

So education is for all, boys and girls; they all have the right to an equal chance to prepare for God's kingdom. In my view education of the very youngest children is by far the most important place to begin such a task. Young children are in a sense least 'corrupted' by the world and, as I said right at the beginning, they are the 'seed' in which the future is mysteriously hidden. If we teach them early, we have a better chance to train the young minds in the way of God.

RO   This is very interesting, for I am in total agreement about the importance of learning – that's why I have schools for the young children and also insist that when the children begin working in the factory from ten years old they still go to school for a period each weekday. And it has never occurred to me to exclude the girls from schooling; after all, they make equally good workers. But for me, this is not so much about preparing for heaven but for preparing for life, life here on earth. So we agree, you can say that Robert Owen and Jan Amos Comenius this day agree that early education is important and that all children should benefit! As for its ultimate purpose – well, maybe we shall have to meet again to talk about that complex question!

PS   OK, so you agree that early education is important, but why should young children go to school? Can they not learn in other places, at home for instance? Schools for the young were introduced by each of you in your different circumstances and centuries but why did you each do that? How do you propose schools are able to contribute to the education of young children?

RO   From my point of view it is about making education part of the community – I need the parents and the older children in the mills, working. The young children need to learn, so I built a school where they would be safe, where they would learn the things I believe are important to them for later life, and where they would have an experience of well-being.

PS   I guess that in the 1980s your school for the younger children might well have been seen as a forerunner of what was called 'workplace nurseries', where companies provided education and care facilities for their employees who were parents.

---

[18] Comenius, *The Great Didactic of Jan Amos Comenius*, p. 67.

RO In my time it meant that young children were safe, doing something useful and not playing on the streets without supervision.

JC Can I respond to this? For me schools have a very important role to play in the learning of men and women, although they are not, in my opinion, the only place that education takes place. As I have said: '*The whole of life is a school*'[19] not just in terms of the time between when we are born and when we die but also in terms of what we experience while we are here on this earth. Learning can and should take place in the home, in the church and in the fields or any place where we work. In my opinion, the home has a special and significant role to contribute to education, especially when the mother is present during the first six years of a child's life.

PS Perhaps some of what you are saying connects with the ideas of 'home education' and even with Rudolf Steiner? Interesting ... perhaps we can pick these things up in another conversation. However ... throughout this conversation you have talked about the 'triangular' relationship between Nature, Man and God. Do you see any similar relationship actually supporting what the educational process is attempting to do?

JC Yes. We'll leave Steiner's ideas aside for now ... But, if we return for a moment to the issue of 'freedom' versus 'control', which we have both alluded to in different ways ... as children are given more freedom to decide upon the actions they take, then I believe there is an increasingly visible relationship between '*knowing* things', '*reasoning* and *speaking* about those things' and then '*acting* upon those things'.

PS How does what you have just said relate to schools?

JC Schools should be places where this relationship of 'knowing' then 'reasoning and speaking' and finally 'doing' is encouraged to develop through appropriate teaching and learning methods. I should add that using resources that are supportive of a child's particular stage of intellectual and emotional development are important in this respect too. Schools, if they operate well, should be almost like workshops where crude or rough pieces of wood are fashioned into beautiful pieces of polished furniture.

PS So children need to be 'shaped' according to someone else's idea of what is beautiful? Is such a concept in danger of being likely to be corrupted? Schools could surely find themselves subject to control from 'outside' and in the noble pursuit of educational excellence suddenly find they are 'manufacturing units of production' rather than 'fashioning works of art'. For example, some would argue that recent policy requirements on curriculum and assessment and teaching styles in English schools, view children as subjects of control from the outside. With such a philosophy as you are suggesting, isn't that where schools function like workshops and education just becomes very utilitarian? Do you recognise this as a danger?

---

[19] J. A. Comenius, *Comenius Pampaedia or Universal Education*, ed. and trans. A. M. O. Dobbie (Dover: Buckland, 1986), p. 58

JC From what I understand of recent policy requirements on curriculum and assessment and teaching styles in England, children already are subjects of control from the outside as you put it. It seems to me that there is much more emphasis in English educational policy on, to use your words, 'manufacturing units of production' rather than 'fashioning works of art'. There will always be those in 'positions of influence' that may have a difference of opinion to our own. Indeed, Mr Owen here is in a position to control what happens in his schools, so it is important that he remains true to the benevolent philosophy of 'respect' in his schools if they are not to control and corrupt children. Power can corrupt – history has shown this time and time again. Yes, there are dangers but we need to be prepared to defend our version of things as we hold them to be true. I accept that this is a risk that has to be taken. As with any progressive step forward there is always a chance that the result might be a retrogressive slip backwards. That should not deter us.

RO I agree. I have 'bought' the opportunity to control the education for these children in New Lanark and my other schools, and yes – I can control what happens there, who teaches there, what they teach … But power need not be evil … in fact, we say that God has the 'power and the glory' so power need not be bad. Power to educate is a responsibility so those who have the power must use it with humility, responsibility and conscience. Reverend Comenius reminded us at the beginning of this discussion that the 'burden of responsibility lies with those entrusted with the care and nourishment of children'. Indeed, you also reminded us that according to Nutbrown all those who work with children need to be 'respectful educators'.

PS This is a fascinating exploration! I'm struck by how ideas connect, for different reasons, how they come from different beginnings and also how ideas recur at different points over time. We're coming to the end of our time for this meeting, but I'd like to draw our conversation to a close by asking you both if you really do believe there is a place for an actual *philosophy* of early childhood education? I'm thinking about the importance of 'protecting' essential elements of early education as I see it, also in ensuring successful early education provision in the future. What do you think?

JC I think I have made it clear in what I have said, how inseparable education must be from a distinct and determined philosophy of what it is for and how it should be accomplished. Without a doubt, a philosophy of early education is essential at any point in time, in any part of the world. My own travels confirmed for me that children, wherever they live, must learn. Without a firm philosophical foundation the future looks bleak, because that is when corruption or a distorted view can creep in.

RO Philosophical basis … yes – I think this is true in what I have established. There is a clarity about why my schools exist, why the young children attend and why the teachers teach what they teach. It is important to know what underpins what is done.

PS   Philosophy of education is now a marginal subject (if it exists at all) in many early years training programmes, so this could be a danger, it could leave the curriculum and a sound pedagogy of early years vulnerable. We need to keep a vigilant eye on this in the twenty-first century.

OK, we talked earlier about how each of you believes that education has a significant contribution to make to the improvement of the individual as well as society. Can we bring our conversation to an end with each of you giving a summary of your educational philosophy? Why do we educate young children?

JC   Yes, I can summarise my beliefs in this respect. The word I use is 'Pansophy' or 'Universal Wisdom'. Firstly, I should say that this means viewing the world or even the universe as a unified whole in every respect. It means accepting that all human activity is linked together or integrated. By this I mean both spiritual activity and material activity not just human 'knowledge' as some would have us believe. Secondly, a pansophic view of the world requires that we use the learning that we have gained through education for the benefit of humanity and the improvement of all aspects of life, and not simply just for utilitarian purposes.

RO   As I have said, education must be a way of nurturing respect for individuals and for ensuring that communities have a cohesion whereby there is well-being, and harshness is shunned. Education is about bringing out the maximum potential of people who will become contributors to the local economy and who will play a part in the smooth running of an industrial community.

PS   And what a responsibility for the teacher! I can identify – in what Comenius has said – many of these things I have myself been observing in young children and reflecting upon with regard to my own practice for some time now. Things like growth, nurture, human potential, carving into a thing of beauty. Reflecting on what you have said I feel, on the one hand, that our discussion has made it easier for me to articulate my own views but at the same time it has also put into stark relief the task entrusted to all of us who educate young children. I'm challenged, too, by Robert's view of early education as an economic necessity but can also relate to the important role of education in alleviating poverty and being central to a local community. I think, overall, I take from our conversation a sense of overwhelming responsibility ... would you agree?

RO   Correct! It is! Teachers have a great responsibility, for young minds, to prepare children for the future and to be kind and fair to them all. And they are powerful too, in a different way – a different sort of power from mine! – but they are the powerful adult in the classroom and so yes, you should be daunted!

JC   It is not daunting if we rely on God and always keep in mind our purpose. I think it underlines the responsibility we all have to each other to ensure we do the best we can for the young children whom we teach. My philosophy is based upon that which is clearly 'working' in the natural world around us. In the same way that a seed cannot be forced to grow, I believe that a child cannot be forced to learn. It is also true that if young children are treated with the respect they deserve, I am convinced a child will blossom into the flower he or she was created to become.

PS   Robert Owen and Jan Amos Comenius, I have been honoured to talk with and learn from you. Thank you.

RO   A pleasure, teach well!

JC   Indeed, my honour too. Teach always with God in mind!

Around 1924, the *British Journal of Psychology* carried the following, uncharacteristic, notice:

WANTED – an Educated Young Woman with honours degree – preferably first class – or the equivalent, to conduct education of a small group of children aged 2½–7, as a piece of scientific work and research. Previous educational experience is not considered a bar, but the advertisers hope to get in touch with a university graduate – or someone of equivalent intellectual standing – who has hitherto considered themselves too good for teaching and who has probably already engaged in another occupation.

   A LIBERAL SALARY – liberal as compared with research work or teaching – will be paid to a suitable applicant …

The advertisement was placed by Susan Sutherland Isaacs, founder of the experimental Malting House School, Cambridge 1924 and 1927.

(Source: *International Journal of Psycho-Analysis* 31 (1950), 279–85.)

Conversation 3

What motivates young children to learn?

An imagined dialogue where
Susan Sutherland Isaacs (SI) talks with **Peter Clough** (PC)

It is September 2007. New curriculum plans have been drawn up and disseminated in England for the teaching of children aged from birth to five years. A new kind of professional is being recognised and awarded Early Years Professional Status. The education of the youngest children remains at the forefront of policy developments and investment in provision for the education and care of young children continues to be made. Targets have been set for provision and for achievement of young children following the Early Years Foundation Stage. There have been continued concerns over the formalisation of the curriculum and of the 'top-down' pressure on young children to learn. But what is it that really motivates young children to learn?

In this imaginary conversation **Peter Clough** talks with **Susan Sutherland Isaacs** about her experimental work at the Malting House School and her beliefs about learning and the role of teachers.

PC   OK, well thank you for agreeing to meet and talk. I've been thinking about young children's learning and this notion of 'motivation' – what makes them tick as learners ... I was reading some of Comenius's work and he seems to hold to a notion of the teacher as 'gardener' and the child as a sort of 'seed' to be nurtured[20] and in that idea there is an implicit relationship between the 'gardener' and the 'seed' – the teacher and the child. His thesis would be, I

---

[20] 'Is there any who denies that sowing and planting need skill and experience? ... the trained gardener goes to work carefully, since he is well instructed, where, when, and how to act and what to leave alone, that he may meet with no failure.' Comenius, *The Great Didactic of John Amos Comenius*, translated in Keatinge 1923 p. 111.

think, that given the right environment, motivation can be an intrinsic as well as extrinsic factor. But I don't think we have really got to the bottom of this idea of 'motivation' when it comes to young children learning, do you?

SI Well, Comenius would argue, I think, that the issue of motivation in young learners is a significant one; he would say that too many young children are denied the intellectual and emotional growth they are capable of and therefore not only their own lives, but also those of society in general, are robbed of a great inheritance. Robert Owen was saying something similar when we talked together of New Lanark and the school there. But I think we must consider motivation as something from the inside. It's there – in young children – all young children – a deep desire to do, to create, to learn, to explore. What happens then is that this motivation can be nourished and encouraged to promote learning or it can be dampened and expunged – as so many earlier teaching techniques have done. You only have to watch young children play and you can see their motivation for learning. And the right teacher, the skilled and intelligent teacher, knows when to add that something extra to fuel their learning. For example, this is how I put it in the publication for the Nursery Schools Association:

> If we are to mention one supreme psychological need of the young child, the answer would have to be 'play' – the opportunity for free play in all its various forms. Play is the child's means of living, and of understanding life ... He needs opportunity for imaginative play, free and unhampered by adult limits or teachings, just as much as he needs and the chance to run and jump and thread beads. It is in this regard that our understanding of the child's mind and the way in which he develops has deepened and broadened in recent years.[21]

PC So is play the real motivator? Do you believe that play is intrinsic? The built-in motivator?

SI Certainly children can generate some interesting scientific questions in their play and then they must find the answers. That's why the teacher must be an intelligent woman and why observation is so important in helping us to plan teaching. And I think it is a mistake to believe that young children should be treated so gently that they always have their own heart's desire – play alone is not what I advocate. I think there should be a toughness ... yes a tough edge to learning – children must think and teachers must be more than gentle-minded mothers. 'They need more than mother wit and mother love; they need true scientific understanding'.[22] Sometimes education must be unsympathetic and make a situation where children struggle in their learning – if they are really keen to know, then they will seek the answer to their own questions. But

---

[21]S. S. Isaacs, *The Educational Value of the Nursery School* (London: The Nursery Schools Association of Great Britain and Northern Ireland, 1954), p. 23.

[22] ibid., p. 30.

I think too that education can be progressive, and at the same time provide direct instruction but there is no need in these early years for a prescribed curriculum.

PC   There's a lot there – can you give me an example?

SI   My observations show that children can, in the right kind of challenging environment, pose for themselves the most complex of scientific questions and good teachers can then help them to find the answers to those questions. Now if we think, for example of the work of John Dewey,[23] we see that it is demonstrating, seeing and knowing and doing that lead to understanding – not pure, abstract instruction. This is a much more useful way of examining learning and of helping teachers make real scientific judgements about how to teach active young minds.

PC   Some might say that the environment you created at the Malting House was one which contained a lot of risk – Bunsen burners, bonfires, all kinds of living creatures, laboratory samples preserved in jars … You emphasise the scientific, the place of 'discovery', as it were, and the role of teachers in encouraging the scientific thinking of young children; today's early years settings would ban most of those things as too risky, and putting the health and safety of children in danger …

SI   And perhaps I would say that the sanitised environment is not one where *real* learning can happen. At the Malting House we aimed to create an environment which included social realities as distinct from fantasies.[24]

PC   Real live encounters with real life things, discovering the wheel? Is that perhaps what really motivates children? Have we got to the bottom of what *actually* makes them *tick*?

SI   Much education of young children wastes opportunities. And from what I see today there is too much readiness to take on 'accepted' practices without thinking about the circumstances in which learning takes place. Teachers should be well-qualified thinkers, graduates, with a scientific mind and capacity continually to adapt their methods to circumstances and to individual children's needs.

PC   Do you think that early years teachers – I should say early years practitioners – do not take into account the needs of the children they work with?

SI   I'm saying that young children need adults who understand about young minds but also have a good knowledge themselves, can impart information, encourage enquiry in lively inquisitive minds – yes … motivate their learning.

PC   OK, before we look at the question of what teachers might do at a practical level to motivate young children's learning, I'd like to put your experience into some sort of context. Susan, you trained to be a teacher in the early part of the twentieth century and entered the profession with a background in psychology as well as education, psychoanalysis too, I believe – in other words,

---

[23] John Dewey, *My Pedagogic Creed* (Washington, DC: Progressive Education Association, 1897).

[24] S. S. Isaacs, *Intellectual Growth in Young Children* (London: Routledge and Kegan Paul, 1930), p. 33.

with a critical and scientific training. Thinking about your work and the Malting House experiment, would you agree that there might be too many teachers who do not critically examine their practice for one reason or another?

SI   Well yes, of course yes! In my opinion it is the prime responsibility of a teacher to observe closely the children and to learn from them in such a way that how they teach and what they teach is tailored to the individuality of each child. And part of that is intense reflection on what is happening in the children they observe and their own interactions with the children.

PC   In that case how does a teacher begin to balance the need to observe and reflect on a personal level and the need to teach more formally? And what of Monsieur Piaget's belief in the importance of particular age-related stages as a basis for planning in teaching young children?

SI   I am not sure that there is such a clear distinction to be made between the two. Both observation and teaching roles are tightly interwoven in a healthy and fruitful teaching and learning relationship. Although the teacher is the 'guide' in one sense, it could be possible that a child could be a guide in learning too.[25]

PC   But you are very clear about the importance of a well-educated teacher too. Can you say more about the idea of a child *leading* the learning?

SI   Well, as Comenius would say, a teacher who uncritically follows precedent when teaching young children, or indeed any individual child, is very unlikely to teach them as well as someone who is willing to modify their approach in the light of their experiences. My own observations lead me to believe that young children have a natural desire to understand the world around them but they also have a desperate need to be understood by those who are significant in their lives. Obviously parents and friends – and, yes other children too – are examples of such people but so too are teachers – guides in their learning.

PC   Well, to stay with Comenius for a moment and his idea that some teachers seemingly work a great deal and achieve proportionately very little ... He suggests that there are times when children can benefit from teachers who consciously seek to 'do' less. Do you, like Comenius, believe that a great deal of learning takes place in the minds of young children when they are left to discover their world uninterrupted by the teacher?[26] If I think about my own work, when I watch young children in a classroom they seem, often, quite

---

[25] 'The grown-ups who are tending little children need to have a sense of fitness and proportion, to know when to give and when to withhold, when to see the baby in the child, and when to respond to the man that he is to be.' Isaacs, *The Educational Value of the Nursery School*, p. 22.
[26] 'Let the main object of this, our Didactic, be as follows: To seek and to find a method of instruction, by which teachers may teach less, but by which learners may learn more; by which schools may be the scene of less noise, aversion, and useless labour, but of more leisure, enjoyment and solid progress ...' Comenius, *The Great Didactic of John Amos Comenius*, translated in Keatinge, 1923, p. 4.

attuned to their surroundings, to the physical and emotional environment. And I think there are particular kinds of environment which promote children's ability to learn. Yes?

SI Say more, what kind of environment would you create? Physical and emotional, tell us ...

PC Well, first of all the adults are crucial, I think; their attitude to the children is key for me ... friendliness, interestedness, warmth ... And then, I think boundaries and rules and expectations. They're important too aren't they – to avoid a sort of 'chaos' ...? And others emphasise too the layout of the room, what's available – they don't agree; Montessori,[27] for example, and her planned experiences, and Nutbrown[28] with the idea of 'workshops'. Much is written about what a place of learning for young children would look like – so there must be a level of importance in the physical environment ... But I think young children, first and foremost, need emotional security in a nursery environment and that's about people and continuity, routine, knowing where you stand, who's going to pick you up if you fall, that you don't eat cabbage – that sort of thing. In any early years environment these things have a huge impact on children's well-being which in turn has to affect their interest, their motivation to do things, to ... to learn. Some children can't wait to get to nursery or playgroup or whatever; others are just not there yet – still very happy at home thank you with their own things, whatever they might be. And so it's relationships that are important in learning; that's true of adults too, even at university, even at PhD level – getting on with your supervisor, tuning in, that's really vital in the motivation stakes. I think it goes without saying that all of us, adults as well as children, are more motivated if we feel confident in, about ourselves.

SI Yes, but I need to say something ... Before a child even comes to school, it is important to consider that they have already learned a great deal in the home environment. Perhaps the most important thing a child has realised is that they have a place and an identity, they have relationships within a family and, of course, they are beginning to understand a little of what they can and cannot yet accomplish on their own. And this connects with our comment about the relationship between self-confidence and motivation in children's learning. It is my opinion that the provision of an environment that meets the emotional needs of a young child as they make the transition from home to school is fundamental in enabling a young child's intrinsic motivation to learn – to flourish in an uninterrupted way.

PC OK, a fluid transition from home to school, and an emotionally supportive environment, but what should the place look like? What do you consider important for the adult to do in a practical sense to ensure that

---

[27] M. Montessori, *The Absorbent Mind* (Wheaton, Il: Theosophical Press, 1964).
[28] C. Nutbrown, *Threads of Thinking: Young Children Learning and the Role of Education*, 3rd edn (London: Sage, 2006).

young children are as motivated to learn in the early years setting as they were at home?

SI   Well, I don't agree with this 'rationed' environment – that wouldn't happen at home, but I would add that I think it's necessary not to underestimate the importance of extending such qualities to the outside environment. The outdoors is often sadly neglected as a learning environment. And despite many projects and pioneers of such things as 'Forest Schools'[29] there is still a lack of real knowledge from the adults and a lack of will from some adults to really make maximum use of the outdoors. Young children's confidence in themselves is promoted a great deal by being given space to simply run and jump and express themselves freely and enjoy games with other children too.[30] But more than that – the outdoors is a natural science classroom. You'll see from some of my work quite how much was learned by interested children in the outdoor school garden and a keen-witted teacher.

PC   So the environment is important, and the adults, but what else? How can teachers really encourage learning? I've worked for a while in my time as a teacher with children with learning difficulties, some really keen but others really disaffected, disinterested – they'd lost it along the way. What can early years education do about that?

SI   I think Jean Piaget would say that it is the development that is important; damaged development in the early years will set up these difficulties. And, yes … I agree, but whatever the circumstances – even where children are struggling – we must return to the idea that teachers need to observe children carefully to establish what the next step is in this process of learning independently. This goes for any learner, whatever the age – you have first to understand what the learner can do, what interests them, and then teach them from that point, not some assumed point according to their age.

PC   This seems to bring us back to the idea of teachers being a sensitive 'guiding hand', much like that gardener nurturing growth from a small seed …

SI   Absolutely. Once a child begins to feel confident or, put another way, has established themselves in the social environment of school, the skill of promoting independence in learning becomes a very high priority in my mind. Perhaps somewhat controversially, I would advocate giving young children a relatively high degree of freedom to satisfy their curiosity and express themselves in the context of broad learning experiences. But there must still be

---

[29] http://www.forestschools.com/phpBB2

[30] 'In general, our aim should be to give children as many opportunities of free movement as possible, and to make use for social purposes of their love of doing things.' S. S. Isaacs, *The Nursery Years* (London: Routledge and Kegan Paul, 1929), p. 71.

teaching ... Child Development theories seem to be sadly lacking in the training of early years teachers and the new Early Years Professionals of the twenty-first century in England. I do not fully agree with Monsieur Piaget's position on developmental stages and their prescribed ages, and we have corresponded at length on these ideas. But I do agree that teachers – indeed all who work with young children – must have a sound knowledge of Child Development theories and be able to draw on these theories to develop high quality and challenging teaching and learning encounters with young children.

PC   Say some more, would you, about the degree of freedom you think children should have. There have to be limits, don't there? What does your version of 'freedom' in early education look like?

SI   Freedom, yes. Well, first of all, freedom comes with good behaviour. The teacher should not condone anti-social and aggressive behaviours that go counter to the 'pleasant' atmosphere that we have agreed is important for young children. I do believe, however, that young children should be allowed to express themselves fully and if such behaviour leads to conflict with other children or adults, then it is the teacher's responsibility to address such behaviour constructively. That is an opportunity for children to learn something too. In my view, such things as aggressive behaviour should be seen in the context of, and at the same time part of, a young child's emotional development.

PC   This makes sense, but you seem to be saying that your position on 'freedom' in the early years classroom is somewhat controversial. It's not *that* liberal, is it? Isn't this something that Charlotte Mason has also pioneered?

SI   That's true, but 'freedom' for learning is a source of controversy because many would say that too much freedom for the young child is either physically or morally dangerous or at least an abdication of responsibility on the part of the teacher. Some religious leaders who have had a hand in the development of schoolrooms for the poor children take the attitude that discipline is a pathway to morality.

PC   'Spare the rod and spoil the child' ...

SI   That is an ethic of some establishments, but not mine. Indeed, some foresighted individuals like Robert Owen also had this belief that physical punishment was not helpful to the development of citizenship. However, I would prefer not to set limits on children's impulses that are governed by adult expectations of respectability and pedagogical purpose. I would prefer instead to set sensible rules for the safe and social behaviour of children which do not inhibit learning.

PC   You really have tested the boundaries of what is acceptable though, haven't you? For example, to have, in that famous account from the Malting House School, allowed – even encouraged – a group of children who were curious to find out if the rabbit was really dead. You let them test a theory about whether it was really dead or not by letting them put it into water to see if it floated. The following day, after a discussion with two boys, you actually encouraged them to dig the rabbit up to see if it was still there! I recall a conversation about this observation in early 2000 when the practitioners I was working with were aghast at this practice! Some were quite appalled. How far would you push the bounds of acceptability to satisfy children's curiosity? What would you say to those practitioners who insist that your rabbit stunt was a step too far?

SI It wasn't a step too far! Absolutely not! And it was not a *stunt*; it was a serious attempt to respect and develop young children's genuine interest and to research with them their very genuine and serious questions. They had a theory that the rabbit was not there – I wanted them to use the evidence available to research the answer to that question. Firstly, I would argue that such examples of allowing young children greater freedom to learn will lead them to discover the truth for themselves and not some 'sanitised' version that we adults often try to satisfy them with. What is equally important though is that as teachers we are at the same time fully exposed to young children and therefore more able to make informed and accurate assessments of their all-round development.[31] And those who work with young children must be knowledgeable and grounded enough to be able to take such questions from children and work with them to find the answers; if that means digging up dead rabbits, then that's what it requires!

PC Can you say a bit more about why this notion of 'freedom' is so important in young children's motivation to learn? It's fascinating …

SI My view is that everything young children do springs from the deep desire within them to learn from and understand the world in which they find themselves.[32] It goes without saying that this will sometimes lead them into behaviours that will challenge not only their boundaries of knowledge but also some people's view of what is acceptable for young children to do. That we must live with …

PC But you draw the line in the sand though, don't you? You don't accept anti-social behaviour. What boundaries did you draw for the Malting House teachers when they observed behaviour which we might call 'unacceptable'?

SI OK, well, to repress such behaviour – purely because it does not 'fit' with our adult understanding of how to behave – to me demonstrates a failure to try to fully understand young children. Young children long to explore, to discover and to understand and as teachers we should accept the challenges that it will bring to our relationships with those we teach. Only by working in this way can teachers honestly say they are being responsive and reflective educators engaged in

---

[31] 'I myself happen to be interested in *everything* that little children do and feel.' S. S. Isaacs, *Social Development of Young Children* (London: Routledge and Kegan Paul, 1933), p. 19.

[32] 'The thirst for understanding springs from the child's deepest emotional needs, a veritable passion.' Isaacs, ibid., p. 113.

motivating and encouraging independence in young children's learning. But yes, there are boundaries which have to be drawn in the interests of acceptability and the good of all.

PC   Some would say that freedom in learning needs to be handled carefully as it has its pitfalls as well as its obvious advantages. One person's freedom is another person's prison.

SI   There will never be agreement on that, but what I am certain about is that these observations now speak for themselves. Readers can now decide if what the children in the Malting House were learning was useful, honest, true scientific understanding. That is one thing I hope to have achieved. Let the records speak for themselves.

PC   Indeed – and thank you for a fascinating conversation.

SI   My pleasure, Professor.

Principles for the Development of a Complete Mind: Study the science of art. Study the art of science. Develop your senses — especially learn how to see. Realise that everything connects to everything else.

Leonardo da Vinci (1452–1519)

I must study politics and war that my sons may have liberty to study mathematics and philosophy. My sons ought to study mathematics and philosophy, geography, natural history, naval architecture, navigation, commerce, and agriculture, in order to give their children a right to study painting, poetry, music, architecture, statuary, tapestry, and porcelain.

John Adams (1735–1826),
former US president

Conversation 4

How do young children learn?

An imagined conversation between
Johann Heinrich Pestalozzi (JHP), **Jean Piaget** (JP) and **Friedrich Froebel** (FF)

It is a winter afternoon and three men meet in a small smoke-filled café overlooking the Schaffhausen Falls in Northern Switzerland, on the Swiss/German border on the Rhine. A waiter ensures that their cups are filled with hot coffee from time to time and the three men talk and talk ...

In this imaginary conversation **Johann Heinrich Pestalozzi**, **Jean Piaget** and **Friedrich Froebel** are talking together about how young children learn.

FF   So, Pestalozzi, I know you are convinced that 'learning through activity' is essential for early education; tell me more about your work which I so admire ...

JHP Definitely sir! My experience with young children leads me to appreciate the necessity of allowing learners to discover the world through activity rather than through direct instruction. I don't accept that young children should be given answers to satisfy their curiosity but encouraged to arrive at them for themselves. Mrs Isaacs would agree with this!

FF   Mmm ... So how do you see this working out in practice? What do you tell those teachers of young children in your schools to do?

JHP Well, in my view, learners, especially young children, are not able to assimilate words as a primary means for understanding a particular concept. What they need is plenty of opportunity to use their own senses to see, to touch and to feel in order to begin to discover what meaning things have for them.

FF   So words or talk of any kind are secondary to practical handling of objects. Is that how you would see it?

JHP   To a degree Froebel, yes, but not altogether. My ultimate goal is the education and well-being of the whole child and so to neglect language completely at any stage would be quite ridiculous! However, my studies have led me to adopt a method or doctrine that seeks to ensure that there is some form of sequence to the process of learning.

FF   Go on …

JHP   You know the German word '*Anschauung*' meaning '*sense perception*' … this implies that direct, concrete observation precedes any form of verbal description of an object.

FF   Many would not disagree with you. Some would put it in terms of 'from the simple to the complex' or 'from the concrete to the abstract'.

JHP   Yes and furthermore, as we progress and mature as learners and as human beings, we discover that our experiences and learning are less and less based in physical or 'concrete' realities. I believe that encouraging young children to begin their learning through the senses is in keeping with their desire to discover and will ultimately produce a balanced learner or – put another way – learning through the hands, the head and the heart.

FF   From what I understand of the work of Steiner, he would not disagree with you there; it's certainly something that I feel is very important as you know.

JHP   Yes, teachers must have a reflective attitude if they are to encourage such a valuable quality in the process of children's learning. This is not always easy and some of the teachers in my own schools found this difficult too. Imaginative teaching situations must be reflected upon, explored and evaluated, first mentally and then verbally. But tell me Froebel, you used the term Kindergarten, 'Garden of children'; it will doubtless become a common enough term one day, used all over the world and attributed to your work with young children. How do you see the role of the teacher and the teacher's relationship with young children in this 'garden'?

FF   I firmly believe that children should be 'nurtured' as are plants in a garden. As you have already said they need a sensitive and responsible 'guiding hand' to help them flourish. In addition, I would also support the view that learning is a natural part of a young child's character.

JHP   Paint a picture of this 'garden'. Tell me how the teacher in the kindergarten is 'sensitive' and nurturing?

FF   Well, I have drawn on your work first and foremost and I also agree with Comenius's view that every child is an individual. Each child develops at their own individual rate and it is most important that the teacher is not only aware of this, but does everything possible to take it into account, when helping young children to learn. In my view this begins by acknowledging that education is a process and the learning that a child goes through is like the process of growth that a seed experiences in fertile ground.

JP   I must interject here, and say that I find all this fascinating Froebel, I'm sure, and the Reverend Comenius would no doubt be pleased to hear you say these things. So would you say that this growth must be cultivated and not artificially forced or, as some might say, rushed?

FF   Exactly Piaget, you and I may not entirely agree on everything here, but I say that each child, like each seed, has the potential for growth inside and just as it is not natural to force growth upon a seed, in the same way it is not natural to impose learning on a child from the outside. I know that this imagery is very strong too in Comenius's writings about the development of young children.

JP   But you don't surely mean therefore that ... that the teacher is a 'passive' participant in her relationship with the child? Surely you are not suggesting that teachers stand back, wait for the 'sun' to come out and then watch the flowers grow in the garden?

FF   No. And you know I'm not saying that Jean. Seeds need more than sunshine to grow. They need water in sufficient quantity and a suitable environment, including opportunities for shade from too much sunshine at times. As I said earlier, each child, like each seed, needs to be given individual attention, and this work of teaching is such a difficult job to get right for each individual child.

JP   Right, but Pestalozzi here asked you to paint him a picture of this garden – what would I find if I were to visit this Froebel kindergarten of yours? What is this 'suitable environment' for teaching young children?

FF   Well, let me put it this way, and this I will read to you, here ... I said, in *The Education of Man*, that simple playthings are important ... things that allow children to 'feel and experience, to act and represent, to think and recognise'.

> *Building, aggregation, is first with the child, as it is first in the development of mankind, and in crystallization. The importance of the vertical, the horizontal, and the rectangular is the first experience which the child gathers from building; then follow equilibrium and symmetry. Thus the child ascends from the construction of the simplest wall with or without cement to the more complex and even to the invention of every architectural structure lying within the possibilities of the given material.*[33]

So you see, the environment is perhaps the most significant factor in the healthy growth of any natural, created being. Food, water and warmth are all necessary but so too is the provision of physical space and adequate time. In my experience children take time to develop, sometimes slowly and in certain respects, sometimes quite rapidly but always it is a process that unfolds from within. Now, I consider it the teacher's role to identify this 'unfolding' and neither to rush nor hold back its development. Yes ... and each one will have required a different type of relationship with the teacher in order to develop as much as possible while they are being taught.

JP   I can see that, and as we have been discussing the importance of relationships, it has brought to the surface something that Mrs Isaacs put to me

---

[33] F. Froebel, *The Education of Man* [1826], p. 281.

in a letter from her Malting House School. It made me think that … in a sense the teacher–child relationship is the 'ultimate environment' if you like, in which growth of the individual takes place. Vygotsky would doubtless have something to say here … as I interpret his work he would argue that real learning takes place when the teacher and the child are in tune with each other – this 'Zone of Proximal Development' of his is where he says the real learning happens. Now the Malting House has all the attributes of a carefully planned and richly stocked physical environment, and these are, if Mrs Isaacs' observations are anything to go by, obviously important.

JHP I'm going to interrupt you because I have to say, my good man, I must say that so much more significant than the physical space is the 'space' for the relationship that the teacher is able to establish with the learner. Froebel here is right on this …

FF Yes, without that important relationship a teacher cannot be expected fully to grasp a young child's individual needs and what the next step in their development requires for the learning process to move forward. For instance, returning to the analogy of the growing 'seed' again, it would be considered unnatural and ultimately destructive if the gardener opened a tender bud with his or her fingers in order to see the beauty of the flower inside.

JP You two keep talking about the importance of teachers being sensitive and 'nurturing' an individual child's natural impulse to learn. But tell me Froebel, what is your opinion regarding the assertion that a young child's natural desire to learn can have both positive and negative outcomes?

FF Well, you know of course that this is an issue that is rooted in our perception of whether young children are fundamentally 'good' or 'bad' as it will inevitably bear a heavy influence on our point of view. Our perception about human nature can lead to different opinions about the form of any relationship a teacher develops with a learner. Such opinions are often, although not entirely, the result of our own experiences with young children. Let me put it this way – this is how I expressed it in my book …

> *The purpose of education is to encourage and guide man as a conscious, thinking and perceiving being in such a way that he becomes a pure and perfect representation of that divine inner law through his own personal choice; education must show him the ways and meanings of attaining that goal.*[34]

JP So you say that they must 'become' pure and perfect, but are they naturally 'good'? Do they need your 'guidance' in this respect?

FF Well, I could ask, does the existence of serious psychological problems for a young child make them any less fundamentally 'good' than those that at least appear to

---

[34] Froebel, *The Education of Man*, p. 2.

conform to 'reasonable' behaviour expectations? Children are made in the image of God – but all men have sinned. I believe that children – well, all human beings – are of essence productive and creative – and seek harmony with God and his world; they seek 'goodness'. Children are born with a need to play and explore, and this they should do. But Piaget, you will have your own observations on what we have been discussing; you have particular views on what young children are capable of learning before they are six years of age ...

JP   Well, if you read Comenius's work and his assertion that learning is more than just the transfer of knowledge ... For me knowledge does not come from the 'outside' in some ready-made form that can be impressed upon the receptive learner like a stamp is stuck on a letter before it is posted ... But I will tell you my position ... My observations of young children learning, as well as those who are older, confirm for me that learners must actively *construct* knowledge for themselves. Human beings are not born with knowledge and they do not gain it by being passive recipients. In my opinion all forms of intelligence, even abstract thought, has its origins in actions of various degrees. Learners tend to 'incorporate' or 'assimilate' new experiences in a way that provides some form of continuity to their existing structures of understanding. At the same time they also 'accommodate' new ideas in a way that expands their understanding and works for change and growth in cognitive development. The term I have used in my work to describe the interrelationship between these two aspects of learning is 'Adaptation'.

FF   I'm following you but I need you to tell me what this looks like for the teacher.

JHP   What Piaget means is ...

JP   I think I'd prefer to utter my own words myself Johann, if you don't mind! I will tell you what it means ... A good example is the imaginative play we often see young children engaged in although it is rather more an example of the tendency to incorporate or 'assimilate' than 'accommodate'. Nevertheless, a child playing imaginatively with an object like a cardboard box clearly shows that young children can play according to their needs at that moment. The box can become a house, a car or a bed regardless of the actual characteristics of the box. The box fits and 'reinforces' the child's current knowledge base as opposed to imaginative play in a 'home corner' of a classroom. Such play would be more an example of a child wanting to accommodate their understanding of an adult domestic scene at home, into their own personal life with friends at school. In this instance a child's development is being 'stretched'; although, I should say that both examples contain elements of these two components that enable learners to construct knowledge.

FF   So when you raise the question of what young children are capable of learning at certain ages or stages of development, what would you say to others – Comenius, Vygotsky, Isaacs, Mason – who hold the view that before the age of six young children can, in the right environment, learn a great deal?

JP   My conviction is that there is a pattern of development in human cognitive processes that follows a sequence and the main stages of that sequence follow one another. Each stage builds upon the previous one and can only begin to do so once the previous one is fully developed within the learner. These stages are generally visible at certain ages in a child's life, although they are not rigidly fixed and indeed there are likely to be exceptions to the general 'rule' that I propose.

JHP And Froebel's three- to five-year-olds – where would they fit into your scheme? Where do they come in your sequence?

JP Well now, let me explain ... I have termed the period from 18 months to 11 or 12 years as the 'Concrete Operational Period' and within that long period I see two distinct phases. I consider a child of the age you are referring to as being within the first of these two phases, the one that generally finishes at the age of seven.

JHP Steiner would perhaps share a modicum of agreement there – he believes that seven is an important age too, but his reasoning does not concur with yours. And what would be the implications for their learning in this phase according to your views?

JP Right, well ... let me see ... I have termed this the 'Preoperational Period'. This phase follows the 'Sensori-Motor Period' and it is characterised by evidence that a child is able to represent things for himself. For example, a child of less than two or three who is asked to put some objects in a row, and then move them before rearranging them back into a row will think sequentially about the practical processes involved. One will follow another. This is evidence that the early processes of 'internalisation' are going on in the child's mind.

FF But how does this relate to your understanding of what young children of this age are capable of learning in the way that Isaacs suggests they can?

JP I see ... Well, my studies lead me to the conclusion that this process of internalisation is not sufficiently developed until the age of about seven or eight for the child to begin to show evidence that he or she can think other than subjectively about things.

JHP But there is evidence to the contrary – surely you see that Jean? Are you implying that you consider that children before the age of seven or eight are basically egocentric and therefore unable to consider another person's point of view? Preposterous!

JP That is precisely what I'm arguing ... Certainly. I would argue the case that a child in the 'Preoperational Period' is not capable of the mental 'flexibility' that older children and adults bring to their learning. And there is nothing 'preposterous' about it! It follows that an egocentric view of the world is, in my opinion, a limiting factor in a young child's ability to 'construct' knowledge in the way I describe.

FF Now, let me see if I fully understand what you're saying here ... In one important respect what you have said supports Comenius's view that young children need to experience the world in which they live on a 'first-hand' or concrete level. That fits with my own position which draws on Pestalozzi's own work. I doubt such a way of learning is questioned by many and certainly none of those with whom I have discussed this particular issue. My own experience, too, supports the view that allowing young children to learn through concrete experiences makes a powerful contribution their development. Mrs Isaacs' work shows the same in my view.

JP   But we have to be clear about the theoretical basis on which we make decisions about young children's learning and not to waste the time of the teachers who seek to have them do things beyond their capacity.

FF   This is fascinating, but very annoying at the same time ... I have another question ...

JP   Sorry my dear fellow, I must take my leave, but let us meet again, and I will take pleasure in more conversation ...

JHP   Farewell Jean!

JP   Au revoir messieurs!

FF   Yes, until next time ...

I felt the tragedy of the working class: to be held back by lack of money from sharing the education of the rich middle class. I also had a sense of what it would mean for social progress if we could support a new educational endeavour within our factory ...

Emil Molt (1876–1936), co-founder of the Steiner-Waldorf Education System, from Molt, Email Molt and the Beginnings of the Waldor School Movement: Sketches from an Autobiography (1919)

I struggled through the alphabet as if it had been a bramble-bush; getting considerably worried and scratched by every letter. After that, I fell among those thieves, the nine figures, who seemed every evening to do something new to disguise themselves and baffle recognition. But, at last I began, in a purblind groping way, to read, write, and cipher, on the very smallest scale.

One night, I was sitting in the chimney-corner with my slate, expending great efforts on the production of a letter to Joe. I think it must have been a full year after our hunt upon the marshes, for it was a long time after, and it was winter and a hard frost. With an alphabet on the hearth at my feet for reference, I contrived in an hour or two to print and smear this epistle:

'MI DEER JO i OPE U R gRWrTE WELL i OpE i SHAL soN B HhBELL 42 TEEDGE U JO AN 7HEN wE SHORL a sO OLODD hN wEN i M PRENOTD 2 U JO wOT LhRX flNBLEvEMErNFxNPrP.'

There was no indispensable necessity for my communicating with Joe by letter, inasmuch as he sat beside me and we were alone. But, I delivered this written communication (slate and all) with my own hand, and Joe received it as a miracle of erudition.

'I say, Pip, old chap!' cried Joe, opening his blue eyes wide, 'what a scholar you are! An't you?'

Pip's account of learning to read and write, from *Great Expectations* (1861) by Charles Dickens (1812–70), novelist

Reading is not a duty, and has consequently no business to be made disagreeable.

Augustine Birrell (1850–1933), author and politician

Conversation 5

Literacy in the early years: a pedagogy of patience?

An imagined conversation where
Rudolf Steiner (RS) talks with **Cathy Nutbrown** (CN)

The time is now ... GCSE results are, again, better than ever before, but there still remains concern over literacy and employability of some young people for whom GCSE was not a realistic proposition. The poor spelling of some undergraduates has been highlighted in the *Observer* newspaper.[35] Worries continue over the literacy levels and the reading habits of boys.[36] For some time government policy has been to begin the formal teaching of literacy earlier and earlier. In the early years new resources were issued for Foundation Stage educators as part of the 'significant steps in the drive to raise standards and personalise learning so that all our children achieve their full potential'.[37]

There remains a lack of agreement about when it is best to begin teaching young children to read and write and in this imaginary conversation **Cathy Nutbrown** talks with **Rudolf Steiner** about what constitutes appropriate literacy pedagogy in the early years.

---

[35] Anushka Asthana, 'Undergraduates let down by week spelling and, punctuation', education correspondent, *The Observer*, Sunday 12 August 2007.

[36] Sarah Crown and agencies, 'Education secretary arranges boys' bookshelves', *Guardian Unlimited*, Wednesday 16 May 2007.

[37] *Letters and Sounds: Principles and Practice of High Quality Phonics*. Issued for local authority advisers, Key Stage 2 teachers, Key Stage 1 teachers, Foundation Stage practitioners, June 2007. Reference: 00281–2007FLR-EN. Quotation at http://www.standards.dfes.gov.uk/primary/publications/literacy/letters_sounds

CN The teaching of literacy has, in my experience, always caused controversy. There is perpetual disagreement about what should be taught, when it should be taught, and how. In my research I've always subscribed to the 'put a book in their hand before they can walk or talk' approach. I do believe that immersing young children with books, inculcating in them a love of books and stories, is a fundamental building block to later literacy learning. But I know the approach taken in Steiner-Waldorf schools, particularly in the kindergarten, is different; you don't encourage the use of books or the formal teaching of reading and writing in the kindergarten, do you?

RS Well, this is an opportunity for me to explain our thinking in the Steiner-Waldorf schools. What I must say first of all is that teachers must understand why human beings need certain circumstances at particular times in their life and the time before about seven years, before the child's second teeth come, is different from the time after that. And they need to be taught with this in mind. Before the adult teeth come children are very much of the body – physical selves ... I can speak only of the most important aspects of body, soul and spirit, in such a way as to give direction to education and teaching.[38] I would direct you to my lectures for the detail of this, for I cannot in this brief exchange convey all that it is necessary to know in order to explain why teaching reading too early is dangerous, counterproductive.

CN Well, many would not disagree on the dangers of formal learning too early ...

RS In the first seven years of life a child learns to walk, to speak, and to think ... If you try to arouse curiosity in a child about some particular word, you will find that you thereby entirely drive out the child's wish to learn that word.[39] Children should come to school around the time of the changing of the teeth, around seven years old. Before that, the home with their mothers and then the kindergarten is the place for them. But when they come to school, your teaching must not be made up of isolated units, but all that the children receive must be a unity ... If they are taught to read and write as two separate things, it is just as though the milk they drink was separated chemically into two parts – it would no longer be milk – no longer pleasant to drink. Reading and writing must form a unity. You must bring this idea of unity into being for your work with the children when they first come to school.[40]

CN So you think that children should not begin school at five (or before five as it is in many cases), and your rationale, if I can put it simply, is that their bodies and souls are simply not ready yet, and that is something that cannot be hurried. Is that a fair way to summarise what you are saying?

---

[38] R. Steiner, *The Kingdom of Childhood: Introductory Talks on Waldorf Education* [1924] (Hudson, NY: Anthroposophic Press, 1995), p. 5.

[39] ibid., p. 12.

[40] ibid., p. 15.

RS In short, that is what I am saying, but I think teachers must understand *why* children are not ready; they must understand what lies behind this, and they should be able to share this knowledge with the child's parents.

CN And reading and writing you see as two sides of the same coin? I think this would echo what was once called a 'whole language approach' where meaning in reading and expression in writing were the focus above accuracy and separate skills, which would be taught and acquired later.[41]

RS I think we are not quite on the same wavelength here, and this is why ... You are seeking to make sense of what I say by matching my ideas, partially, to your own experience – just as children do! But the key thing is that what is done in the classroom – and not done in the kindergarten – is the rational for the doing or not doing. This is not so much about repeating particular practices but of understanding *why* those practices are important and then knowing how to respond in the classroom with the children according to their needs. Let me explain ... The calligraphy of today is quite foreign to children both in written or printed letters. They have no relation to an A, for example. Nevertheless, when children come to school they are taught these things, and consequently the child has no connection with what he is doing.[42] And if they are made to, say, stick letters into cut-out holes before the time is right for them, they are asked to work outside their nature. It is difficult for them and they are at odds with their learning.

CN I think this fits with the work of Bredekamp on 'Developmentally Appropriate Practice',[43] but again – the rationale is different from your own.

RS What you should appeal to is what the children do possess – an artistic sense, a faculty for creating imaginative pictures ... You should avoid a direct approach to the conventional letters of the alphabet that are used in writing and printing.[44]

CN This notion of readiness is an issue, whatever form of pedagogy or whatever particular approach to early education is taken. But literacy is so important, and there is this climate now of young people struggling with literacy. Employers sometimes complain that new employees are not fit to work because they cannot read instructions, write a letter, or add up accurately. There is a fear that starting too late can cause literacy difficulties and many of us who have carried out research in early literacy have met this concern and we have to keep trying to reassure that

---

[41] K. Goodman, 'Reading: a psycholinguistic guessing game', *Journal of the Reading Specialist* 6 (1967), 126–35. And also N. Chomsky, *Language and Thought* (Wakefield, RI and London: Moyer Bell, 1993).

[42] R. Steiner, *The Kingdom of Childhood*, p. 23.

[43] S. Bredekamp, (ed.), *Developmentally Appropriate Practice in Early Childhood Programs Serving Children from Birth through Age 8*, expanded edn (Washington, DC: NAEYC, 1987).

[44] Steiner, *The Kingdom of Childhood*, p. 23.

starting too young is not necessarily the way to ensure a grasp of literacy early.

RS People will object that the children learn to read and write too late. This is said only because they do not realise how harmful it is when children learn to read and write too soon. It is a very bad thing to be able to write early. Reading and writing as we have them today are really not suited to human beings until a later age – the eleventh or twelfth year – and the more a child is blessed with not being able to read and write well before this age, the better it is for the later years of life.[45]

CN I think I would have a problem with that – eleven or twelve seems very late. Certainly if a child can't read reasonably fluently by then they would be considered to have learning difficulties. And wouldn't these children struggle with the rest of the curriculum? Literacy is the key to the whole curriculum – struggling with literacy throughout the school years means struggling with the whole of schooling.

RS But perhaps, then, it is the nature of the schooling that is wrong, not the child.

CN Ah! OK, so I'm perhaps not allowing myself to think sufficiently radically in this conversation. I need to imagine a system of education and pedagogical practices which are truly based on what we know of children, child development and humanity. And then I need to imagine a society which is similarly constructed.

RS Well, naturally you really wouldn't be able to proceed as I suggest because children have to pass from school into adult life,[46] so there has to be some accommodation. But it is important to know these things – the child who struggles is not struggling with reading but struggling because the time when he is being asked to learn these things is wrong for him.

CN So what can I take from the Waldorf approach that can realistically be transposed into an early years setting or a Key Stage 1 classroom? Can it be possible to have a part-Waldorf approach?

RS I would prefer things were done properly rather than piecemeal, as I said earlier – things fit together as a whole with the child in terms of body, soul and spirit. But let's think about how letters can be taught … Go to a Waldorf school and you will see teachers teaching letters in all kinds of ways – forming the shapes with string, painting different shapes and forms from which letters eventually arise, letting children 'dance' the forms of the letters around the room – experiencing the shapes with their whole bodies … There is freedom for teachers to be creative, but there is not chaos, because the spirit that is appropriate for each child is active in every class.[47]

---

[45] ibid., p. 27.
[46] ibid.
[47] ibid., p. 29.

CN   These are echoes too of the multi-sensory approach to literacy teaching which is popular with some early years teachers and also used with pupils with learning difficulties.[48]

RS   And why do they have difficulties? Maybe because they were asked to learn these things too early!

CN   Well, there are many reasons why children struggle. I do agree that too much too soon can be detrimental. I believe that early literacy experience, like other aspects of young children's learning in the early years, can be gained through play. And in my work with Peter Hannon and Anne Morgan, we have shown how parents can provide 'Opportunities', 'Recognition', 'Interaction' and 'Models of literacy users'.[49] We've shown that parents really value the chance to learn more about how their young children learn literacy.[50] We've also looked at how important the role of stories and talking together are in families and in early years settings. In fact it was Gordon Wells's work which showed that listening to stories has an impact on later reading achievement.[51] It is important, wouldn't you agree, that children are told stories, made up stories, again and again?

RS   It is of course important, but I don't attach this importance to later reading success. I see it as important because it is what the young child needs. Indeed in Steiner schools you will hear teachers telling stories right through the school. Telling stories, often with a large picture, which they themselves have drawn on the blackboard ...

CN   Gosh! That really takes me back to my own infant school days ... Sometimes we would come in from lunchtime play and find a huge picture filling the board and the teacher, Mrs Condon, would say, 'if we get our work done I will tell you the story that goes with this picture before you go home'. I loved her stories, and I was amazed that she could draw those huge pictures in coloured chalk ...

RS   That is not uncommon in Steiner classrooms, but you will often find that the story comes at the start of the day. Steiner-Waldorf teachers must be good story-tellers and good illustrators! But I must make a point here about the stories told to young children – we must not just tell them any story. Different kinds of stories are fitting for different ages of children according to their needs of body, soul and spirit. This is important – not until the age of nine do children see themselves as separate from their environment. For this reason, everything around little children should be spoken of as if it too were human.

---

[48] See J. Taylor, *Handwriting: A Teacher's Guide – Multisensory Approaches to Assessing and Improving Handwriting Skills* (London: David Fulton Publishers, 2001) and also H. Schupack and B. Wilson, *The "R" Book: Reading, Writing and Spelling: The Multisensory Structured Language Approach* (Baltimore, MD: The International Dyslexia Association's Orton Emeritus Series, 1997).

[49] C. Nutbrown, P. Hannon and A. Morgan, *Early Literacy Work with Families: Policy, Practice and Research* (London: Sage, 2005).

[50] P. Hannon, A. Morgan and C. Nutbrown, 'Parents' experiences of a family literacy programme', *Journal of Early Childhood Research* 3(3), 19–44.

[51] G. Wells, *The Meaning Makers: Children Learning Language and Using Language to Learn* (London: Hodder and Stoughton, 1987).

Plants, animals, stones should be spoken of as if they too can speak, love, hate. Anthropomorphism should be used in the most inventive ways.[52] Treat all things that feel and live as if they were human, and allow trees and stones, sun and rain and wind to talk — everything you bring to a child of this age is like a fairytale.

CN   So the fittingness of anthropomorphism would, if we subscribe to your theory, explain why I loved the *Velveteen Rabbit* and the Beatrix Potter tales of Peter Rabbit and others.

RS   These are the proper things for children, young children, to hear. They can hear the other tales of human strife and love and hate and all later — the Greek myths and legends, the Old Testament stories, all of those come later when the child is ready in his body and soul to take them. You must teach and educate out of the very nature of the human being,[53] and for this reason education for moral life must run in parallel to the process of teaching which I set out.

CN   From my experience of visiting Steiner schools, it seems all the teachers are such good story-tellers — they tell such compelling stories ...

RS   When telling stories everything depends on the art of telling. Word-of-mouth narration cannot, therefore, simply be replaced by reading.[54] The teachers must learn how to tell stories, and know the stories in their hearts, and tell them as if they were real, believe the truth of them ...

CN   Your focus is education for life, isn't it ... part of a process of learning to be human? I can see this, but many policy-makers would not be content with this view. We inhabit a world of targets, success, failure, achievement, and so on, and because of that success in early literacy learning is crucial ... Can the Steiner-Waldorf approach really be successful in this kind of policy context?

RS   The teacher must come into the classroom in a mood of mind and soul that can really find its way into the children's hearts.[55] Any other approach will be damaging. It is, however, extraordinarily difficult, in view of what is demanded of children today by the authorities, to succeed with an education that is really related to life itself. One has to go through some very painful experiences. Once, for instance, because of family circumstances, a child had to leave the Steiner-Waldorf school when he was about nine years old. He had to continue his education in another school. We were then most bitterly reproached because he had not got so far in arithmetic as was expected of him there, nor in reading or writing. They said that the painting and other things he could do were of no use to him at all.

CN   But if he could not read at nine years old, he surely was at a disadvantage in the state school, yes?

---

[52] Steiner, *The Kingdom of Childhood*, p. 31.
[53] ibid., p. 52.
[54] R. Steiner, *The Education of the Child: And Early Lectures on Education* [1924] (Hudson, NY: Anthroposophic Press, 1996), p. 25.
[55] Steiner, *The Kingdom of Childhood*, p. 62.

RS   Professor, let me put it this way ... If we want to educate children out of knowledge of the human being and also in accordance with the demands of life, they will need to be able to read and write to the standard expected of them. So the curriculum will have to include things because they are demanded.

CN   Do you think the gender of the child was significant in his later development in literacy? There has been growing concern that boys take longer to achieve certain aspects of literacy,[56] though in some of my own work boys were involved in literacy at home. At the age of five, the boys in our study were active in literacy, even if studies and national testing raise concerns about literacy not being a masculine pursuit and boys' achievement in literacy later being lower.[57] Working-class boys seem to be the group that struggle.[58]

RS   Boys and girls are different. Girls grasp things more easily than boys and with greater eagerness too.[59]

CN   So how about giving boys different, more boy-friendly reading material, about football, cars, that kind of thing? The boys in our study really enjoyed their books, the illustrations, talking about them with their fathers. I can't see that this is harmful. But this emphasis of yours on only *telling* stories, not *reading* or encouraging reading in the kindergarten, does not fit with my experience as a nursery teacher or as a researcher.

RS   Professor, we shall disagree on some things, but I hope we shall not disagree on this ... However we decide to fulfil the policies of the country and of the time we work in, we must still try to relate the children to real life as much as possible and for little children we must awaken a delight in them ... liveliness, and a happy enjoyment of story.[60]

CN   ... delight, liveliness and a happy enjoyment ... yes! Thank you!

RS   ... and thank you Professor!

---

[56] DfEE, *Excellence in Schools* (London: The Stationery Office, 1997).

[57] C. Nutbrown and P. Hannon, 'Children's perspectives on family literacy: methodological issues, findings and implications for practice', *Journal of Early Childhood Literacy* 3(2), 115–45.

[58] P. Connolly, *Boys and Schooling in the Early Years* (London: RoutledgeFalmer, 2004).

[59] Steiner, *The Kingdom of Childhood*, p. 119.

[60] Steiner, *The Education of the Child*, p. 25.

I sometimes wonder if the hand is not more sensitive to the beauties of sculpture than the eye. I should think the wonderful rhythmical flow of lines and curves could be more subtly felt than seen. Be this as it may, I know that I can feel the heart-throbs of the ancient Greeks in their marble gods and goddesses.

Helen Keller (1880—1968),
American author, activist and lecturer
from *The Story of My Life*, Pt 1 (1903)

For what is Mysticism? Is it not the attempt to draw near to God, not by rites or ceremonies, but by inward disposition? Is it not merely a hard word for 'The Kingdom of Heaven is within'? Heaven is neither a place nor a time.

Florence Nightingale (1820–1910),
pioneer of modern nursing

To see a world in a grain of sand,
And a heaven in a wild flower,
Hold infinity in the palm of your hand,
And eternity in an hour.

William Blake (1757–1827), poet, painter and printmaker
from 'Auguries of Innocence' (1803)

I can very well do without God both in my life and in my paintings, but I cannot, ill as I am, do without something which is greater than I, which is my life, the power to create.

Vincent van Gogh (1853–90),
Dutch Post-Impressionist artist

Conversation 6

From God and Church to awe and wonder: spirituality and creativity in early childhood education

In conversation:
Peter Clough (PC) and **Cathy Nutbrown** (CN), with a note from **Philip Selbie** (PS)

It is summer 2007. New discussions have taken place in the media around the role of faith in education and the place of 'faith schools' in raising educational achievement on the one hand and dividing communities on the other. Violence by and towards young people has given rise to further debate about discipline and respect in education and society as a whole.

In this conversation **Peter Clough** and **Cathy Nutbrown** are reflecting on some of the motives of historical figures and of organisations and institutions which provided education in the past. They are in Cathy's office in Sheffield, surrounded by piles of history books, biographies, papers, archive material and notes. In this conversation they trace education as part of religious conviction and identify key elements which seem to them to be important lessons, and perhaps legacies, for early childhood education in the twenty-first century.

PC   The motive of the Church – to provide education – that goes back to where ... 1700s? Lancaster's Monitorial schools were part of the Quaker movement and the much cited, but not fully understood, New Lanark enterprise of Robert Owen. But it wasn't just about philanthropy or good works for poor people. There was a distinct enterprise on the part of the established Church to teach religion. It's here, in this note about the formation of the National Society, 1811:

> *That the National Religion should be made the foundation of National Education, and should be the first and chief thing taught to the poor, according to the excellent Liturgy and Catechism provided by our Church.*[61]

CN The start of Church of England schools, the beginning of nation-wide education, was only picked up and supported by the State in 1870. In the UK the Church was a key player in developing early education through Sunday Schools and the like … and the need to teach people to be able to read the Bible … A lasting legacy, because there are now around 5,000 C of E schools in England and Wales, most of them providing education for children up to 11 years – around a million children.

PC But it was 1836 … the Evangelicals and non-conformists who promoted the development of 'infant schools', the Home and Colonial School Society.

CN Organisations and movements made a real impact on faith schools but individuals with a religious conviction or belief also were active in providing for young children. The McMillan sisters were surely driven by their Christian Socialist convictions – religious and political drive I think, as well as their own education and 'mission' to do something for young children in difficult home circumstances. Even Florence Nightingale had her say in her letters about what young children should be taught … Here's a copy of her letter from the archive to Alice Hepworth, a teacher (or 'little mother of the infants' as Nightingale puts it). She was 66 when she wrote this. Listen … the whole letter, about 14 handwritten pages, is about the importance of religious instruction for the 'infants' at Lea School in Derbyshire; she asks if they are going to introduce to the children 'the nice lessons practised in Thomas Street … the little moral tales which you used to give your scholars once a week at Thomas St'. And she continues:

> *And would there be time now for giving the religious morning instruction in talk? Perhaps you always do this. I do not know exactly what the Infants' religious instruction is. It may be necessary to give a good deal of learning Scripture by heart. But then if Scripture is really to tell on the children's lives – the only thing that Christ cares about & that Christ came to live & die for – & still lives for – the little 'mother' must explain a good deal by little tales & illustrations.*[62]

There's another letter from her to the School Master William John Prinsep Burton (his wife, Mrs Adeline Burton, was the infants' Mistress):

> *I am delighted to hear the result of the School Scripture Examination – not that a Scripture Exam ensures an earnest life necessarily among the children, any*

---

[61] http://www.natsoc.org.uk/society/history
[62] Letter to Alice Hepworth, dated 9 March 1886, Clendening History of Medicine Library: http://clendening.kumc.edu/dc/fn/2hpwrth1.html

more than a Grammar Exam. But it is a Master's (or a Mother's) daily Scripture lesson, from which the children learn whether he (or she) means it for their life or no – whether it is to bring in 'the kingdom' into our lives, or whether it is merely a lesson in words.[63]

PC   Fascinating ... she took an interest in education, then, as well as medical matters. And the school in Derbyshire was clearly close to her heart. She sent books and bibles ... and made her views quite clear. But this idea of religious instruction, and learning passages by heart being the most likely form of lesson for the infants, we wouldn't do that now ... and it wouldn't be wholly Christian ...

CN   It takes me back to my own days in Sunday School, learning texts by heart. But we didn't do that in school. There would be little of Nightingale's form of religious instruction now, if anything, in the early years ... It would really be more about encouraging the children to develop a sense of awe and wonder about the world. Stories, moral tales. How did Stella[64] approach this, because it would clearly be different in an Independent New Christian school?

PC   Christian schools began a long way back. George Muller – famous for the development of orphanages – also sought to set up schools ... Listen, he writes that one of his aims is ... here ...

> *to put the children of poor persons to such Day-schools, in order that they may be truly instructed in the ways of God, besides learning those things which are necessary for this life.*[65]

But as for the new Christian schools, the accounts in *The Love of God in the Classroom* point to an ethos and curriculum for the youngest children which aims that 'Infants', as they call them, should 'know God through His word and His creation'.[66] Reading this, it's not so far away from the aims of Muller and Wesley:

> *The Christian schools have been forces for good in their neighbourhoods in that they have often been able to help families with needy children, for whom the other schools are not working for one reason or another. Often what is needed is the*

---

[63] Letter to Mr Burton, dated 30 August 1897, Derbyshire transcripts of *Kelly's Directory* from: *Kelly's Directory of the Counties of Derby, Notts, Leicester and Rutland* (London, May 1891), pp. 183–4: http://www.andrewspages.dial.pipex.com/dby/kelly/deth-lea-holl.htm

[64] A former student of ours on a postgraduate programme and a teacher at one of the new Christian schools.

[65] Dated 7 October 1834; B. Miller, *George Muller: Man of Faith and Miracles* (Minneapolis, MN: Bethany House, 1941).

[66] S. Baker and D. Freeman, *The Love of God in the Classroom: The Story of the New Christian Schools* (Rosshire, Scotland: Christian Focus, 2005), p. 93.

loving atmosphere that a Christian school is uniquely able to provide. What better environment for any child than one where the love of Christ is known and felt? ... The Lord Jesus promised that, where his people were meeting in his name, he would be present in a special way, and that is the testimony of the schools and of those who visit them.[67]

CN And these New Christian schools are very different, aren't they, from the more traditional 'faith schools' like the Church of England or the Roman Catholic schools?

PC They're often worlds apart as far as the religious commitment of pupils, parents and staff are concerned, however explicit the traditional faith schools might be about their mission ...

CN Perhaps the point is that it's more than a curriculum, it's a mission to teach children about how to live, to have a belief, a set of values ... based on a religious doctrine. But there is the argument that segregated education systems bring about division and breed misunderstanding and contempt ... and all that parliamentary argument in 2002 when the government planned to expand state-funded faith schools and were defeated.

PC These debates have made leaders of faith schools come together and address such criticisms of segregation and division in communities. This is from their joint statement about community cohesion:

> *We will work together to further our shared commitments to:*
>
> - *excellence in all our schools*
> - *enabling all children to achieve their full potential*
> - *celebrating achievement and valuing people*
> - *developing effective partnerships between home, school, and the wider community.[68]*

And that's a statement endorsed by representatives of many organisations of faith-based schools issued in 2005.[69] But this is a long way from Nightingale's letters about scripture lessons, and the pioneers of Church schools of the 1800s. I've been thinking quite a bit recently about this element of faith – well, Christianity mainly – that is so central to a lot of the thinking of our pioneers ... Well, for some of them – and perhaps Comenius is the best example – a belief in God is absolutely central to their pedagogy ... No – more than that: for

---

[67] ibid., p. 16.

[68] http://www.teachernet.gov.uk/wholeschool/faithschools/statement

[69] Methodist Church, Board of Deputies of British Jews, Association of Muslim Schools UK, Network of Sikh Organisations, Seventh Day Adventist Church, Agency for Jewish Education, Church of England, Greek Orthodox Church, Catholic Education Service, Churches Together in England.

someone like Comenius you couldn't even start to talk about early childhood education as something independent of a theology ... an expression of a Divine scheme ... the rearing of children in godly ways, yes?

CN   Ah, yes, and Comenius really stressed the purpose of education as making humans fit to become like God, and therefore education had to be of a form that would treat children in ways which would help them, too, to become like God. Here, he wrote ...

> *Children ought to be dearer to parents than gold and silver, than pearls and gems, may be discovered from a comparison between both gifts of God; for ... Gold and silver are fleeting and transitory; children an immortal inheritance.*[70]

PC   Exactly! That's what I'm saying ... God is central to the pedagogy that is being put forward. I wish Philip was here to help us with Comenius, but we'll see what he says later ...

CN   But when you say that God is central to the pedagogy, where does that take you?

PC   So, suppose you don't believe in God – and let's face it most, well many don't – then is the Comenius stuff any use? I mean if you strip out the core wiring – as it were – that carries the religious current, does his work truly have any contemporary appeal?

CN   You mean, is there still an important pedagogy without an appeal to God? Well there must be; I've worked with countless brilliant teachers – I mean really brilliant – who are not remotely interested in religion. In fact some who were vehemently opposed ... sort of 'Keep God out of the Classroom!' But they would all accord with Comenius's views about play and learning, about the importance of nature, his idea of 'opening up their understanding to the outer world' ... The rationale might be different, the philosophy which drives the pedagogy, but the belief in the importance of a holistic approach to pedagogy, a respect for the child, those things would be recognisable, and I think it's important in the twenty-first century to take these ideas of the past, like Christian Schiller said, and make them our own, forge new paths ... and I don't mean throw away the old stuff. But in a world where for many, many people God is not the reason for life and living, we have to find different points of reference ... well we have to be free to do that ...

PC   Yes, I see that, and agree, I think – but perhaps some of the teachers you talk about would acknowledge something more like spirituality ... if not *God* and *faith*?

CN   And if I think about little children, for me, it's not so much Nightingale's urge that they should learn passages of the Bible by heart, or the catechism as it might have been in times gone by. Although, having said that, I still recall some

---

[70] J. A. Comenius, *The Great Didactic of John Amos Comenius* [1657], translated into English and edited with biographical, historical and critical introductions by M. W. Keatinge (London: A. & C. Black, 1923), p. 34.

of the words I learned in Sunday School! For me, in present times, early child-hood education should be about teaching children to wonder, to experience awe and wonder in the world ... yes, a kind of *spirituality* in themselves. That's why I like the opening words of Blake's poem, 'Auguries of Innocence':

> *To see a world in a grain of sand,*
> *And a heaven in a wild flower,*
> *Hold infinity in the palm of your hand,*
> *And eternity in an hour.*[71]

And to draw on Comenius:

> *The proper education of the young does not consist in stuffing their heads with a mass of words, sentences, and ideas dragged together out of various authors, but in opening up their understanding to the outer world, so that a living stream may flow from their own minds, just as leaves, flowers, and fruit spring from the bud on a tree.*[72]

Little children can do that; they really can see a world in a grain of sand, they really can be open to the world, like leaves, and flowers ... And we interrupt them all the time – 'hurry up, come on' we say, rushing them on when what they want to do is peer long and hard into the grass to watch an ant in the soil, or watch waves crashing on a rock ... I have a photo of a little girl holding a leaf and there's a ladybird on the leaf. In her three-year-old's face you can see puzzlement, intrigue, but ... yes awe and wonder. That's what I think we need to make sure is so very present in early years provision, and it's one of the reasons why I worry so about the downward pressure of curriculum for older children which seems to have the effect of squeezing out the arts.

PC   I can see what you're saying but there's so much to untangle here. Do we need to draw some distinctions between teaching a faith, and teaching *about* faiths? 'Cos many of those teachers who'd be opposed to any notion of God-in-the-classroom would be wholly committed to multi-culturalism, multi-faith educa-tion, celebrating Eid or Holi or whatever ... teaching respect for different cultures, the importance of people, children, families of all faiths and none and being informed about the practices and traditions of different faith groups. But *spirituality*, that's different isn't it?

CN   It is, and there's an important point here I think. Now I know some faiths wor-ship in very simple surroundings, in simplicity and silence in some cases. But many faiths make their places of worship awesome! Even if that is at the expense of people in the community who live in real poverty. Look at some

---

[71] Blake, W. (1917) Auguries of Innocence in C. W. Eliot (ed.) 2001, *English Poetry II from Collins to Fitzgerald* (New York: P. F. Collier and Son).
[72] Comenius, *The Great Didactic of Jan Amos Comenius* p 92.

of the cathedrals, mosques, synagogues, temples … they are beacons of beauty, art, craft … Why does the Church invest in the best of choral music; huge organs with the most accomplished of organ scholars; stained glass, ancient and modern – wonderful works of art, using colour and light to make you gaze, kneel in wonder; and in elaborate vestments – the clergy adorned in gold, red, purple, heavy embroidery? Because the Church, 'high church', knows how to use colour, words, sound, music, art, touch, scents even, to create a sense of wonder.

Now I'm not saying that art equals spirituality, but I am saying that building up and encouraging young children's sense of awe and wonder and creativity is a way of helping them to think and wonder and puzzle about other amazing things later, like God and beliefs and life …

Look at all the people who visit some of the famous cathedrals in the world, light candles even, many of whom declare themselves as non-religious. But what does this mean – apart from being able to say 'I've been to Notre Dame'? The architecture, music, paintings, stained glass, sculpture – for those who created these buildings, stone by stone, year after year after year – are great monuments to the glory of God. For me, spirituality and creativity go hand in hand. That's why the arts are so important – a sort of channel of expression of what's in one's soul. And yes, spirituality, awe and wonder can be about and connected with belief in God, but they don't have to be … And it's important that whatever a family's religious faith or non-belief might be, every child's early years give them opportunities to wonder and gaze and take in amazing things. To quote Socrates, 'Wisdom begins in wonder'.

PC So learning begins with little children being fascinated with their world?

CN I think what matters most of all is that we be aware of some reason for doing what we do: not 'Well, we do it this way because that's how it's done here', or 'Because that's how I was taught to do it in college', but 'We do it this way because we believe that children learn better if …' or 'We do it this way because research shows that children …' You know? You should be able to justify everything – I mean every single thing – you do in a setting …

PC You mean like a … a fully-worked out theory? A philosophy?

CN Yes … theory, philosophy … but it may be religious belief of one sort or another. In any event, it's an *ideology*. For Christian-based education it's underpinned by 'Jesus said: "*Suffer the little children to come unto me, for of such is the Kingdom of Heaven*"; and then there's St Paul: '*When I was a child I spoke as a child … But when I became a man I put away childish things …*' These two texts collide really … Christ saying children are perfect; Paul saying that the aim is to get through childhood and grow up! But I can see how approaches to teaching young children could be based on views of childhood such as these. And how you see children, no matter how that view is derived, will determine (to some extent) the shape of provision and practice, and research for that matter.

PC You mean it could be based on a political view of childhood?

CN Not necessarily – though any view must be! No, rather ideology simply as an organised collection of ideas, a distinct way of looking at things, a means of justifying one's thinking and practice. Practice has to be based on something, belief in something and for some it's belief in God, for others, social justice ... for some it's both, and more.

PC   So, how do you get, in your thinking, from God and Church to your position on 'awe and wonder' being the approach to developing – or perhaps I should say supporting – young children's spirituality?

CN   Well, I was reading about Vincent van Gogh and Barbara Hepworth the other day and van Gogh's famous words about creativity when he said: 'I can very well do without God both in my life and in my paintings, but I cannot, ill as I am, do without something which is greater than I, which is my life, the power to create.' And then Hepworth who wrote of the importance of her childhood to the development of her ideas: 'Perhaps what one wants to say is formed in childhood and one spends the rest of one's life trying to say it'. If I put these two things together, I come up with a view of how important creativity, the arts are to the human spirit.

PC   And you wouldn't be alone there ... Steiner wrote that 'A sense for what is noble and beautiful awakes love for what is worthy of love. But what strengthens the will is religion; it must permeate the teaching of every subject'.[73] He went on to say that: 'We enter earthly existence through birth and there a creative and productive spirituality takes over the formative material of heredity before we can develop concepts. Only later is the conscious soul added'.[74]

CN   Well, maybe I'm trying to put too many things together, but I do think that spirituality is not necessarily dependent on belief in God or in holding a religious faith. Many would not disagree with me ... What I'm trying to get at in terms of the arts is the way they offer opportunity for young children to experience 'creation' ... Those who have pioneered the arts in education haven't done so on an 'arts for arts' sake' pitch. They've pointed to learning, to self-confidence, to the capacity of the arts to open up young minds to a different kind of thinking. But I want to say that without art we die! Yes, 'Without art we die'. Literally, human beings have to make their mark, draw, dance, sing ... and it's inside us. Some are better at it than others, but all children (unless they have damage in their lives), all children want to dance, paint, sing, make noise, make marks – it's only adults who suppress this sometimes ... this very natural urge. I recall being in the Ulster Museum in Belfast a couple of years ago, with Elliot Eisner[75] and we were looking at some beautifully crafted Egyptian hair ornaments and other jewellery, and he said to me, 'Why do you suppose people make these things?' I didn't realise what he was getting at immediately ... then he said, with that very thoughtful tone of

---

[73] Steiner (1996) *The Education of the Child and Early Lectures an Education.* Hudson: Anthroposophic Press. p. 69.

[74] ibid., p. 112.

[75] Professor Elliot W. Elsner is Professor of Education and Art at Stanford University. Widely considered the leading theorist on art education and aesthetics.

his, 'Because it reminds them that they are human beings'. Human beings must create ... Early education needs to adopt a pedagogy of the arts.

PC   A pedagogy of the arts ... and part of your rationale for that is to foster spirituality?

CN   To foster awe and wonder, and within that, support the development of children as spiritual people, yes. HMI, the 'old' pre-Ofsted HMI – the real Her Majesty's Inspectors – were so good at promoting the arts. Think of Christian Schiller ...

PC   And the work of Robin Tanner ... 'If those we teach are potentially creative they deserve to be taught by artists and craftsmen ...'[76] And Sir Alec Clegg. When you start to think about it all it's quite incredible, the things that were achieved only a few decades ago ... And how regimes and policies can shift emphases in education so rapidly, and even make us forget those deeply significant contributions to teaching and learning ... So how would you sum this up Cathy? How do we achieve an ideology of early childhood education which builds on the best of its roots, adapts to modern times and needs, and still gives children a sense of humanity, awe, wonder, helps them to become spiritually aware people.

CN   It's about love, I think ... and, as I've said before, a belief that teaching little children to love each other is as important ... as important, more important, yes more important than teaching them to read and write.

PC   Love in the early childhood classroom ...

CN   Yes – yes, exactly that – and I know that needs a huge amount of discussion but, as Jools Page says, we should start talking about it![77]

PC   And beginning to develop in children a simplicity of faith and belief, so that we can really talk about respect for young children's approaches to understanding the world ... and I could quote more of Blake's 'Auguries of Innocence' (if I could remember it!):

> He who respects the infant's faith
> Triumphs over hell and death.
> The child's toys and the old man's reasons
> Are the [... something ...] fruits ...

CN   'Are the fruits of the two seasons.'[78] Philip will have a perspective on this ... I'll send him a copy of the transcript, maybe he'll e-mail his thoughts ...

[We did! And Philip responded ...]

---

[76] R. Tanner (1989) The Way We Have Come notes from a lecture to a Plowden Conference 1977.

[77] J. Page (2007) Theorising Love and Care – unpublished Seminar Presentation University of Sheffield.

[78] Blake, W. (1917) Auguries of Innocence in C. W. Eliot (ed.) 2001, *English Poetry II from Collins to Fitzgerald* (New York: P.F. Collier and Son)

A fascinating discussion – wish I was there! But here are my thoughts …

For me, we have to be able to separate the form of a 'religious faith' (the particular and recognisable expression of it) from 'spirituality' (the rather more difficult to define experience of it). I think the two can be (but are not necessarily) related or even dependent upon each other. I might even go as far as to say that 'spirituality' is the common denominator of all religions and a 'place' where humanity begins to enter into the fullness of life that we are all intended to experience.

Actually, I think that perhaps faith (in God) itself begins with being fascinated with the world and the mystery of it all. As you have said earlier, children seem to have a natural propensity to be able to experience this and to not be frightened or inhibited by it in the way that we as adults seem to. As educators we need to somehow protect this quality and yet at the same time not limit it by our desire to preserve it. We need to nurture it and keep it vital and fresh and the avenues opened up by creativity are perfect for this. Real and deep learning surely have their roots in the spiritual dimension and I think young children are more than capable of this given the right environment.

And, yes, I think the thing about experiencing 'spirituality' is that it doesn't have to be connected to a particular faith and also I certainly would not want to say that someone of 'no defined faith' can't experience it either. In fact, very young children who have yet to be introduced to teaching about faith or various forms of it seem to have an immense capacity for spirituality. This is perhaps why, with the purest of motives, people like Florence Nightingale felt that exposing young children to moral stories would help nourish in them that which they believed was already deposited within them from birth. Helping children to engage with things that point to the 'otherness' of human experience is a way of keeping that sense of awe and wonder alive.

One word that comes to mind here is 'innocence'. One Christian view on this is that in that initial state of innocence into which we are all born we have the greatest capacity to love, not only others but God and even ourselves too. (*Though some would probably disagree with me here … if they adopt the belief in Original Sin …*) However, I don't think that being in a state of innocence in this sense means being ignorant or immature either. Quite the contrary actually, because a newborn baby or a young child must automatically possess a great deal of trust on account of their vulnerability and this is what is so important if children are going to love each other. Trust is almost a pre-requisite or pre-condition of love. Humility comes in here too because, I think, if children are going to develop fully as human beings, they need to be able to allow that spiritual dimension to their nature to be exercised. For me things like awe, wonder and fascination just can't happen for us unless we are prepared to accept that there is something 'bigger' than ourselves. One, if not THE most important task of early educators, as Cathy has said, is to help little children to learn to love each other and I think we can begin to do this by helping them to retain the innocence and humility that is part of early childhood.

PS

When I despair, I remember that all through history the ways of truth and love have always won. There have been tyrants, and murderers, and for a time they can seem invincible, but in the end they always fall. Think of it — always.

Mahatma Gandhi (1869–1948),
political and spritual leader of India

History never looks like history when you are living through it.

John W. Gardner (1912–2002),
American politician

History is the witness that testifies to the passing of time; it illumines reality, vitalizes memory, provides guidance in daily life and brings us tidings of antiquity.

Cicero (106 BC–43 BC), Roman statesman,
lawyer, political theorist and philosopher
from Pro Publio Sestio

4 Plus ça change ...?

It is often said that the more things change, the more they stay the same, so in this final part of the book we bring together the present with the past and look at the relation of contemporary issues and policies with their historical precedents. Here we reflect on some of the important contemporary issues of the twenty-first century which affect early childhood education and care, and the nature of such concerns as they affected earlier generations.

But before we take a look at recent and current policies we must draw attention to the labyrinthine nature of policy and policy communication; look at this, for example, a passage from a recent DfES document:

> This document contains the statutory framework for the EYFS [Early Years Foundation Stage]. It sets out the legal requirements relating to learning and development (the early learning goals; the educational programmes; and the assessment arrangements) in Section 2 and the legal requirements relating to welfare (safeguarding and promoting children's welfare; suitable people; suitable premises, environment and equipment; organisation; and documentation) in Section 3. The learning and development requirements are given legal force by the Early Years Foundation Stage (Learning and Development Requirements) Order 2007 made under Section 39 (1) (a) of the Childcare Act 2006. The welfare requirements are given legal force by Regulations made under Section 39 (1) (b) of the Childcare Act 2006. Together, the Order, the Regulations and the Statutory Framework document make up the legal basis of the EYFS. The requirements in this document have statutory force by virtue of Section 44 (1) of the Childcare Act 2006.

Taken from the *Statutory Framework for the Early Years Foundation Stage: Setting the Standards for Learning, Development and Care for Children from Birth to Five* (DfES 2007: 8) paragraph 1.7, this seems to us a typical example of a form of words which is almost impenetrable, certainly opaque and operationally challenging. Navigating such policy, and remaining aware of multiple policy developments, is a full-time task, and unravelling the complex policy connections to reach the heart of an issue and relate it to practice is a challenge of a scale that has never before existed. Our predecessors did not have the weight of policy that exists now and neither did they have instant access to numerous and ever-changing policy statements and guidance that is now available through government websites. In the twenty-first century policy shifts and communication of those policies are faster and more detailed than in times past – for good or ill.

We identify seven themes which we see as recurring throughout the book; these are:

1. Children's rights
2. The Arts and creativity
3. Literacy
4. Play, learning and pedagogy
5. Early intervention
6. Home learning and parents
7. Inclusion.

In the pages that follow we take each of the above issues in turn and reflect on some recent events, research and policies relating to them. These reflections are followed by another look back to the less recent past to identify the work of those who might be seen – however anachronistically – to have been motivated by the issues.

1. Children's rights

Current policy and practice in children's rights in the early years

The United Nations (UN) Convention on the Rights of the Child lists 54 Articles which are designed to prevent illness and neglect; provide education; protect from abuse and exploitation; and ensure participation in decisions that affect them.

Issues of children's rights have gained currency in the last 50 years, beginning with the *Declaration of Rights of the Child* by the General Assembly of the United Nations on 20 November 1959. Subsequently, the UN Convention on the Rights of the Child was established by the United Nations in 1989. The 1959 Declaration established ten principles which laid down rights to which the UN said children should be entitled. These included the right to:

1. Equality, regardless of race, colour, religion, sex or nationality
2. Healthy mental and physical development

3. A name and a nationality
4. Sufficient food, housing and medical care
5. Special care if handicapped
6. Love, understanding and care
7. Free education, play and recreation
8. Immediate aid in the event of disasters and emergencies
9. Protection from cruelty, neglect and exploitation
10. Protection from persecution and to an upbringing in the spirit of world-wide brotherhood and peace.

The language of the Declaration of 1959 is somewhat changed in the Convention of 1989, where 54 detailed Articles define the range of children's rights under four categories. The Convention states children's rights to:

1. *Prevention* (of illness and neglect)
2. *Provision* (of education with specific references to children who are disabled)
3. *Protection* (from abuse and exploitation)
4. *Participation* (in decisions which affect them).

The issues covered under the theme of 'children's rights' is very wide ranging and, internationally, focuses on issues which include such topics as: corporal punishment, child poverty, legislation, child labour, child health (including immunisation, food and the environment). Children whose families are refugees or asylum seekers also have these rights when in a country which is a signatory to the Convention and thus controversy reigns when children in such circumstances are not treated according to the rights which should be afforded to them. Recently, disputes over hospital treatment, allocation of school places and housing have been brought to court on the basis of contravention of the UN Convention on the Rights of the Child.

Recent policy has addressed issues of rights in relation to protection through the *Every Child Matters* initiative (DfES 2005), the National Childcare Strategy in 1998, Sure Start (DfEE 1999), *The Ten Year Childcare Strategy* (DfES 2004), integrated services of protection, health and education, and the *Early Years Foundation Stage* (DfES 2007). Within these wide-ranging policy initiatives many issues of rights are addressed.

Of course, issues of 'rights' have been variously embraced and disputed and different countries take a range of views, as do institutions and individuals. However, where a country is a signatory to the UN Convention on the Rights of the Child, it is required to adhere to, promote and report on progress in implementing the Convention. There are many examples of work to promote children's rights but two are worth some space here.

In Sweden children's rights have been a focus of interest and concern since the UN Convention was signed in 1989. Studies have included work on young children's understanding of their rights and the development of practical materials to help children to learn about the Convention and to discuss their rights (Backstrom 1997). Similar resources have been developed in other countries (Covell and Howe 1999).

A Save the Children study of young children's rights (Alderson 2000) examined children's involvement in decisions which affected them. Based in the UK, the study showed how children's contributions were often unrecognised by adults and how many adults, due largely to their desire to protect children from danger, denied children basic freedoms to play, be with their friends and spend time in the park. Alderson (ibid.) gives many examples of young children participating in decisions about their lives, such as: suggesting ideas for the development of play facilities, buildings and menus; and getting involved in strategies to resolve bullying.

There are examples of practice where children's rights are a fundamental and guiding principle of curriculum and pedagogy. Such an example can be found in the infant-toddler centres and preschools in Reggio Emilia in Northern Italy. Central concerns are:

> The rights of children: the fact that the rights of children are recognised as the rights of all children is the sign of a more accomplished humanity;
>
> The rights of teachers: for the teachers, each and every one of them, it is a condition that enhances communication and the comparison of ideas and experiences, all of which enrich the tools of professional evaluation;
>
> The rights of parents: participation and research are, in fact, two terms that summarise much of the overall conception of our educational theory. These two terms might also be seen as the best prerequisites for initiating and maintaining a cooperative understanding between parents and teachers, with all the value that is added to the educational prospects of the children.

> (Malaguzzi 1996: 2)

A second example is found in the argument of daily practice; that is to say that, though governments which have signed the UN Convention on the Rights of the Child thus formally declare their commitment to it, much of the reality of putting children's rights into practice lies in the hands of individual practitioners working in services and settings for children and their families. This draws attention to the fact that while there are obligations on governments, 'there are responsibilities for every adult citizen too' (Nutbrown 1996: 108).

Such arguments continue to be made, with concerns that too great a focus is still being placed on the UN Convention, on Geneva, and the structure of the Committee on the Rights of the Child and too little on development and progress at a more local level (Veernam and Levine 2000).

Some roots of children's rights

Some may imagine that ideas of 'rights' for children is a new and modern concept. But if we look back through time we can see how, using different forms of expression, the idea that children should have rights is in no way 'new'.

Perhaps Comenius's position in the 1600s on how children should be educated could be viewed as an issue of 'right' because, for him, the child was God given and therefore should be treated as such; in this sense the child's rights were God given. Rousseau's notion of protection of Emile until he was able to think for himself carried underpinnings of this 'ideal' state of education for young children, and while he viewed the education of girls as different from that of boys (because they were being educated towards different 'ends') he nevertheless held the view that girls too should receive education.

A clear example of education as a matter of social justice is to be found in the work of Pestalozzi who, between 1804 and 1806, established schools for under-privileged and abandoned boys and girls, in the belief that education was a key component in improving conditions in society. His direct work with children, including those with learning impairments, is paralleled with another significant achievement in terms of his approach to early education generally: promoting an education of the 'whole' child where teachers were 'sympathetic' towards young children and where children were not forced to conform to adult wishes or ideals. His ideas were developed by Froebel, who also stressed appropriate ways of working with children, and he could be said to be a proponent of a child's 'right to play', an issue which is still troubling some educators in modern times.

Similarly, Robert Owen's approach, also in the early 1800s, was to see young children's education as something which formed a part of society as a whole and fitted with housing, work and health care. His early ban on corporal punishment would perhaps amaze those who today still regard smacking by parents as an appropriate response to 'bad' behaviour. His insistence that teachers treat pupils well could be interpreted as a view that educators should 'respect' their pupils. Rachel and Margaret McMillan worked in the early 1900s to combat ill-health and poverty by providing clinics and centres for children living in the slums of Bradford and in London; their work was self-consciously politically driven and based on a premise that children's success in education and good health were directly linked.

Of all those whose life and work we have reflected on in this book, it is the work of Charlotte Mason that carries the clearest connection to issues of children's rights; her 20 'Articles of Education' have also been referred to as a child's 'Bill of Rights' (Cholmondeley 1960: 227). Mason's work was based on the ideas of Rousseau and Pestalozzi and she developed her own distinctive philosophy of education in which she spelled out exactly how education should be for young children. She described education as 'an atmosphere' by which she meant that children should be part of the real world and not isolated or separate from adults and their daily work and routines. She argued that 'it stultifies a child to bring down his world to the "child's" level' (Mason 1923). This was different from the work of Froebel and Montessori who were in favour of creating 'scaled-down' child-size environments in their Kindergarten and Children's Houses, and is also, no doubt, something which would challenge aspects of current policies and the practices of many practitioners in the Early Years Foundation Stage. Her view was that children should learn through living, that parents should play a central part in their children's early learning – including reading with them, and reading 'good' literature – and that the outdoor world was the best classroom. Her final publication, written in 1923, shortly before her death at the age of 81, includes these words:

> The claims of the schoolroom should not be allowed to encroach on the child's right to long hours daily of exercise and investigation.
>
> Children have a right to the best we possess; therefore their lesson books should be, as far as possible, our best books.
>
> They require a great variety of knowledge – about religion, the humanities, science and art.

Reading Charlotte Mason's writings leaves the impression of a woman whose ideas were distinctly ahead of her time and, despite the different forms of expression, there is much to be found here which can be clearly identified as a pedagogy of rights which would fit well with the work of many educators concerned to place children's rights more centrally in current practice.

2. The arts and creativity

Current policy and practice in relation to present understanding around the arts and creativity in the early years

If we look to developments in Europe we can see, in Scandinavia and Northern Italy, for example, how a focus on the arts can enhance children's learning in all aspects of their development. The now familiar work of Reggio Emilia (Reggio Children 1995) demonstrates how arts-based curricula and experienced support from artists can give rise to learning in all aspects of an early years curriculum. Such projects promote sustained, shared thinking and foster children's learning 'in community'. In Sweden, a physical environment and adult involvement which stimulates and enables children's dramatic play has been shown to enhance young children's imaginations and involvement (Lindqvist 2001).

Studies and projects closer to home have confirmed that the youngest children can respond to, and enjoy, involvement in the arts. Work at Tate Britain for children under three and their parents has shown how artist involvement can open up new avenues for parents to explore and enjoy the arts with their young children (Hancock and Cox 2002). We know also the importance of talk in early years settings and recent research demonstrates the centrality of oracy and storytelling in the early years curriculum (Harrett 2001). Recent arts-based learning projects, including the work of Creative Partnerships, have shown that even short-term involvement of artists can enhance the early years curriculum (Gillespie 2006), and current early years curriculum policy acknowledges the place of the arts in young children's learning (Sure Start 2005).

But how have we come to this, and what role has policy played in reaching this position? During the 1990s the place of the arts and of creativity generally suffered in favour of education founded on the 'basics' which were given prominence by the introduction of the National Curriculum as a result of the Education Act (1989) and later by the Foundation Stage (2000) and Baseline Assessment (1997). Together these policy initiatives had the effect in many settings of squeezing out (or seriously limiting children's experiences of) the arts – even in the early years. Alert to the difficulties this was causing and aware of the potential dangers which may occur as a result of a narrow curriculum, the National Advisory Committee on Creative and Cultural Education (NACCCE) was set up in May 1999 to make recommendations to government on

> the creative and cultural development of young people through formal and informal education: [and] to take stock of current provision and ... make proposals for principles, policies and practice. (NACCCE 1999: iv)

The report recommended education provision, formal and informal, for young people to the age of 16 and for a wider national strategy for creative and cultural education. In anticipation that an emphasis on creativity and culture might distract from raising standards in literacy and numeracy, the report said:

> We are not advocating creative and cultural education as alternatives to literacy and numeracy, but as equally relevant to the needs of this and of future generations. We support the need for high standards of literacy and numeracy. These are important in themselves. They can also enhance creative abilities: equally creative teaching and learning can enhance literacy and numeracy. These are complementary abilities, not opposing objectives. The Government and the vast majority of people in education recognise this. (ibid.: 13)

Recommendations included: raising the priority they give to creative and cultural education; revising the National Curriculum from 2000; and ensuring 'that teachers and other professionals are encouraged and trained to use methods and materials that facilitate the development of young people's creative abilities and cultural understanding' (ibid.: 197). It was arguably the recommendation for partnership that has led to a more embedded approach to the arts and creativity in recent years:

> the development of partnerships between schools and outside agencies ... are now essential to provide the kinds of creative and cultural education that young people need and deserve. (ibid.: 199)

This led, among other initiatives, to the development, in collaboration with the Arts Council, of the 'Creative Partnerships' initiative – goverment's creativity programme for schools and young people, managed by Arts Council England and funded by the DfES and the Department for Culture, Media and Sport (http://www.creative-partnerships.com), which has successfully promoted creativity and the arts in education settings and beyond. For example, *The Secret Garden* project in Stoke-on-Trent[1] involved children and young people collaborating with dancers, film-makers, a horticulturalist/occupational therapist, a zoologist and a sculptor to develop the ideas for the space and innovative experiential sculpture. The *Second Skin* project in Coventry[2] saw children from birth to five developing stimulating learning environments. Working together, 11 artists and 10 early years teachers created multi-sensory environments to explore how children's creative responses could stimulate their creative learning. One participating teacher commented:

> it has re-lighted my creative/artistic side that had been placed on the back burner for such a long time.

So, from the demise of the arts and creativity, there has been a surge of interest in the arts and, perhaps inevitably, a renewed fear of marginalisation and

---

[1] http://www.creative-partnerships.com/projects/200244
[2] http://www.creative-partnerships.com/projects/58577

lowering of achievement in the 'basics'. In 2007, a government minister called for A level students to be 'encouraged' to study mathematics and the sciences, arguing that too few were taking degrees in subjects that 'were necessary to the economy of the country'. However, this was shortly followed by a statement by Prime Minister Gordon Brown who announced that

> because schools are the foundation, we need to ensure all schools are committed to high standards and are at the same time centres of creativity, innovation and enjoyment. Ready to challenge and inspire – fostering scholarship, inquisitiveness and independence of thought, teaching facts and imparting knowledge – of course. But doing far more than that – nourishing all forms of talent – because that is the future of our nation. (Mansion House, 20 June 2007)

While it is not yet the case that the place of arts and creativity is secure in the early years, it does appear that policy currently promotes the arts alongside more traditional 'academic' subjects such as literacy, numeracy and the sciences.

Some roots of present understanding around the arts and creativity in the early years

Creative Partnerships has without doubt achieved great success in promoting the arts and creativity, but there was a legacy to inherit and a secure platform on which to build this work. Between 1885 and 1909 three boys were born who were, in their adult lives, to affect education and the arts in England in a way that no one had done before. Informed, no doubt, by the work of Rousseau, Pestalozzi, Froebel, from the 1920s onwards, Christian Schiller, Robin Tanner and Alec Clegg promoted a change in primary education which was radical and far reaching.

From around 1930, Alec Clegg emphasised the importance of creativity in education, pioneering in-service courses for teachers. Between 1930 and 1974 he personally visited many schools, talking with teachers about their work and developing an extensive collection of children's artwork. He noted that

> there are two kinds of education: the education of the mind by imparting facts and teaching skills, and the education of the spirit, and the material to be worked on here is the child's loves and hates, his hopes and fears, or in other terms, his courage, his integrity, his compassion and other great human qualities. (Clegg 1964: 19)

In his book *Excitement of Writing* (1964) Clegg wrote:

> Children learn mostly from that which is around them, and from the use of the senses. These impressions so gained will depend a great deal on interests which will vary considerably. If children are interested they will listen more carefully, look more closely and touch more sensitively. With interest there is created the element of wonder, the most precious element of life. (17)

Clegg's different and less constrained outlook on learning situations for children inspired many teachers, one of whom was Mrs Muriel Pyrah whose work with children over some 40 years he described as 'unlike anything I had ever seen and indeed I have never seen its like' (Clegg 1980: 7).

Similarly, HMIs Robin Tanner and Christian Schiller worked from the 1930s onwards, promoting creative, and what might be called 'progressive', approaches to education, often through residential courses for teachers which were at the time run by HMI and funded by the Department of Education and Science. In a lecture given to the Plowden Conference in 1977, Tanner describes his partnership with Schiller:

> at a course for teachers in Chester I met and listened to a colleague who was to teach me more than any other – indeed, who has taught England more about Primary Education than anyone else in this century – Christian Schiller ... To him it seemed obvious that the education of children should be centred upon them ... Schiller insisted that in order to learn and grow children must move, try out their powers, explore and find out for themselves. (Tanner 1977: 7)

Perhaps it was Schiller's influence that led Tanner to argue so strongly for a curriculum which allowed children to create. He wrote:

> If we need scientists and technologists we need also gardeners, and carpenters, tailors, artists, postmen, writers, dancers, clerks and booksellers. Man cannot live by bread alone! .... I would emphasise that in young children there is a timeless, primitive, elemental simplicity that it would be folly to try to pass by. And it is children's sense of awe and wonder at the phenomena of the natural world that should be at the root of their scientific investigations. The other world will all too quickly teach them the rest! ... In every school education should be primarily through the arts. (ibid.: 13)

Because of their work and that of others there is a chorus running throughout history which lauds the arts and promotes creativity and discovery as essentials in learning. New generations somehow have to re-discover this truth, but the recurrent theme of arts and creativity in early education stands testimony to what is, we suggest, an indisputable truth: that it is the arts which remind us of our humanity and the arts which offer us ways of expressing that humanity to others.

3. Literacy

Current policy and practice in literacy in the early years

Until the 1970s early literacy development was effectively overlooked; Nursery education tended to focus on oral language and storytelling. Literacy only properly became part of the early years curriculum during the 1980s with the growth of research in *emergent literacy* and a shift from a belief that literacy learning too young could be harmful to the development of practices which incorporated meaningful literacy activities – based on children's everyday lives – into the curriculum. New ways of teaching literacy were developed during the 1980s as researchers and teachers became more aware of *how* children learned about writing and reading. These changes in thinking and practice were also incorporated (to some extent) in the new English National Curriculum in 1988 (DES 1988). Since then, developments have been rapid and now it would be difficult to find settings where literacy is not a key element of the curriculum. Children are also encouraged to use reading and writing in many aspects of their play. The Foundation Stage (QCA/DfEE 2000) promoted the incorporation of aspects of literacy learning through play and required the assessment of literacy according to elements on an assessment scale for *Communication, Language and Literacy* which assessed: language for communication and thinking; linking sounds and letters; reading; and writing. Assessed elements included: using phonic knowledge to read simple regular words; showing an understanding of the elements of stories, such as main character, sequence of events and openings; attempting writing for a variety of purposes, using features of different forms (DfES/QCA 2003).

   In countries where print abounds there is no shortage of examples; commercial print of all kinds can be found on clothing, buildings, packaging, household equipment and so on. It may be temporary and ever changing, as with electronic bill boards and digital screens on shopping centres, cars and transport depots (bus and rail stations and airports for example). Context-based print, such as that found on household packaging and shop signs, is meaningful to young children and has a place in their reading development as children draw meaning from familiar symbols in their environment (Goodman *et al.* 1978; Hiebert 1981). It has been suggested that reading begins the moment young children become aware of environmental print (Smith 1976) and many children develop a sense of such print awareness long before going to school (Goodman 1980; Burke 1982). Environmental print can stimulate talk about literacy as children ask questions such as 'What does that say?' It also prompts children, at times, to pick out and identify from signs some letters that are familiar to them, perhaps in their own name.

Environmental print can stimulate some children to imitate the writing they see, such as notices or notes left for others.

Access to books, especially good quality books, both children's fiction and non-fiction material, is essential if children are to build a good foundation of reading in their early years. Concepts such as the quality of illustration or the overall quality of the story and look of a book are matters for personal judgement, but if children are introduced to the best of what is on offer in children's publishing, they are more likely to want to use them, want to turn the pages, to look at the pictures and listen to the story and to return to the book again later.

Children absorb messages very quickly, both positive and negative, and so the literature offered to children and taken into homes needs to be selected so that it offers positive images of all members of society, of a variety of cultures and of both males and females. The first encounter with a particular book is important, and the cover, the feel, size, shape as well as the content make a difference to whether children and parents are attracted to read it or not. Meek (1982) argues that reading books and stories *together* is the fundamental cornerstone of reading. In recent years there has been a growth of literature for children based on the popular culture of the time. Books related to children's television programmes and films abound and numerous related comics for children are available in most newsagents. Marsh (2005a) has argued that literacy related to children's popular culture should be valued and children's use of texts in comics, films and TV-related story books, television and other multi-media literacies should be a part of children's literacy repertoires.

Some studies (Bissex 1980; Baghban 1984; Payton 1984; Schickedanz 1990) have provided useful insights into the fine detail of children's early literacy achievements and patterns of learning. Research into children's early mark making (Goodman 1980; Harste et al. 1984; Ross and Brondy 1987; Ferrerio and Teberosky 1989) challenged the earlier belief that children could not and should not write until they go to school. As more was understood about 'emergent' or 'developmental' writing, teachers in the early years began to watch what children were doing and incorporate provision and support for such writing behaviours and interests into the preschool curriculum. Ferrerio and Teberosky's (1989) work focused on the hypotheses about writing which children generated for themselves as they tried to understand writing rules and conventions. The children in their study explored various ideas and hypotheses about writing – writing, they argue, does not depend on graphic skill (their ability to make letters look conventional) but on the level of conceptualisation about writing – that is the set of hypotheses they have explored for the purpose of understanding writing.

Three aspects of oral language appear to be key to children's literacy learning and development: storytelling, phonological awareness and 'talk about literacy'. Goswami and Bryant (1990) and Maclean *et al.* (1987) have identified the importance of *phonological awareness* in children's literacy development. Goswami and Bryant (1990) suggested that the important thing for children to be aware of is what they call *onset* and *rime* in spoken words, 'onset' being the beginning sound and 'rime' being the end sound of a word. Their work highlights this importance of *alliteration* and *rhyme* thus showing the role of nursery rhymes in early literacy development. Goswami and Bryant (ibid.) showed that children who are aware of onset and rime find learning to read easier. Maclean and colleagues (1987) found that preschool children's knowledge of nursery rhymes predicted later reading success in school.

Wells's (1987) longitudinal study of children's language in the home identified key experiences. He found that the best predictor of children's reading attainment in school was a measure of what he termed 'knowledge of literacy' at school entry. Foremost of all of the activities found to be important to later literacy achievement was *listening to stories read aloud*. Wells suggested that this was because it extended experience and vocabulary; increased conversation with adults; validated the children's own 'inner storying'; and enabled children to use language to *create worlds*.

Most recently the place of new media and popular culture in children's early literacy development has attracted interest. Television programmes often have accompanying merchandise: dolls, figures, books or comics, lunch boxes, t-shirts, bed covers, wallpaper and so on (Kenway and Bullen 2001). The force of popular culture in the development of children's literacy has been highlighted by Dyson who shows how television 'superheroes' can fuel children's writing (Dyson 1997; 2002).

Some roots of early literacy

It is fair to say that literacy was the reason, or at least a strong reason, for the development of schools. Comenius, in 1658, published *Orbis Sensualium Pictus* (The Visible World in Pictures), believed to be the first picture book for children. Robert Owen from 1816 placed an emphasis on books and reading. Charlotte Mason, working from around 1860, believed that books had a central role in the education of young children but that they should be the best books, not 'twaddle' (her word!) which reduced the world to a simple form, but books which told stories of life and told them well. She might even be seen as the first to champion the cause of the 'real books' movement which became popular in the 1970s!

Religion played a large part in teaching literacy and Sunday Schools were set up for the education of the poor, mainly to teach them to read the Bible (though not to write, since it was not desirable for the poor to be able to express their ideas). Robert Raikes is widely acknowledged for his work in establishing Sunday Schools in the 1780s, for adults as well as children. Raikes was editor of the *Gloucester Journal* and following an article in 1783, the number of Sunday Schools grew, supported in 1785 by the national Sunday School Society. By 1784 there were some 1,800 Sunday School pupils in Manchester and Salford, and in Leeds (Kelly 1970).

But perhaps a lasting legacy in terms of promoting literacy and providing regular and free access to books of all kinds comes from William Ewart, a politician who, in 1850, introduced a bill to parliament which paved the way for 'free libraries' funded by local council rates. Libraries have, over the decades, suffered threats of closure, yet their free status remains and their role in providing books to support study and leisure reading is widely acknowledged.

There have been other identifiable points of influence on the teaching of literacy over the years. Marion Richardson, an Inspector of Art, developed in 1935 the eponymous system for teaching handwriting in primary schools (Richardson 1935). This was followed by an attempt, in the 1960s, to make the teaching of reading to infants less difficult through the development of the 'Initial Teaching Alphabet' (ita) by Sir James Pitman, grandson of the inventor of Pitman shorthand. Though some schools used this system it never became an established method of teaching (though some still promote its use).

The novels of Charles Dickens demonstrate his view on the importance of literacy for the poor and of the place of literacy in 'bettering oneself' in society. Literacy, literacy teaching and literacy difficulties will no doubt remain an abiding theme in the unfolding history of early childhood.

4. Play, learning and pedagogy

Current policy and practice in learning and pedagogy in the early years

As it is understood in early childhood education and care, play is a central component of children's experiences and a key means by which they learn. Defining play is problematic, though the word 'play' is used liberally and with the assumption that its meaning is understood. Play has, in turn, been heralded as the essential means through which children learn (Hutt *et al.* 1989), and then castigated and sidelined in favour of ensuring that young children should 'work' in school. In the introduction to their book *Structuring Play in the Early Years at School*, Manning and Sharp (1977: 7) explain the purpose of their project:

The idea of the project first arose because of the difficulties which many teachers were experiencing in using play in the classroom. Although accepting that children learn and develop through play, and that play is a motivating force for children's learning, many teachers are pressurised by the very full first school curriculum and large classes to neglect play as a means of teaching. They leave children to play on their own. In addition, many parents' expectations are that children will 'work' when they come to school, not 'play' .

Over 30 years later many teachers continue to struggle to 'fit' play into their pedagogic repertoire and, though play now has a newly respected status in the early years, some practitioners still lack the necessary skills, support and confidence to make children's play an integral part of learning and pedagogy. A Working Party of the British Educational Research Association (BERA) reviewed research on early years pedagogy, curriculum and adult roles. The review stated that:

Several key studies have provided an evidence base on the quality of play, its educational benefits, and the pedagogy of play, in the contexts of preschool and school settings (Tizard et al 1975, Sylva et al 1980, Wood et al 1980, Meadows and Cashdan, 1988; Hutt et al 1989, Bennett and Kell 1989, Cleave and Brown 1991, Bennett et al 1997). Most of these studies did not focus specifically on play, but on broader curriculum and pedagogical processes, of which play was an integral part. Their findings were critical of the quality of play; the dislocation between rhetoric and reality of play; the extent to which play and learning were linked; the role of the adults in children's play, and how play was utilised towards educational outcomes. The consistent picture to emerge from these studies is that play in practice has been limited in frequency, duration and quality, with teachers and other adults too often adopting a reactive 'watching and waiting' approach. (BERA EYSIG 2003: 14)

While research evidence is inconclusive, the natural, irrepressible instinct and capacity of children the world over to play and the perceived benefits of play to children's holistic development provide a strong case for the professional exploration of the role of play in supporting children's well-being, development and learning.

In recent years increasing attention has been paid particularly to the play of children from birth to three and this is an important issue for many practitioners. Manning-Morton and Thorp (2004) examine the importance of play for children under three years of age and identify the crucial role for adults in such play in supporting and developing play experiences. Play is seen in relation to all aspects of a child's day, integral to and part of a holistic approach to early education and care for very young children.

Research continues to focus on definitions of play, children's roles and interests in play and how play is supported in various forms of early years provision in a variety of international contexts. But questions about the efficacy of play as a pedagogical tool remain and successive governments show varied commitment to play in the early years and schools curriculum. The implementation of the National Literacy and Numeracy Strategies, for example, promoted the importance of the basic skills and threatened play. Teachers became anxious that as standards were raised play was increasingly sidelined (and in some cases eliminated). Christmas (2005) asked the teachers and other staff in her small village school for their views on play and found that while people generally thought it was 'OK to play', worries over the play/work balance remained.

Themes of children's play are mostly influenced by their experiences – either first-hand or secondary experiences such as those gleaned from television or stories – and the practices of practitioners faced with war and gun play vary from 'zero tolerance' to a strategy of embracing and seeking to enhance the play. Holland (2003) argues that war, weapon and superhero play, properly supported with sensitive adult guidance, can be generally positive experiences for children and practitioners, resulting in imaginative play and social development. Hyder (2004) explores the importance of play for young refugee children's development. She considers the implications of war and conflict on young children and notes how opportunities for play are often denied them. Hyder's work with young refugee children is set in the context of the UN Convention on the Rights of the Child and she argues that play is a healing experience for young children affected by war and conflict.

Some roots of present-day approaches to play, learning and pedagogy

Of course, the names which come to mind when a history of play is discussed include Rousseau, Pestalozzi and Froebel and their contribution permeates this book. But others too have made important contributions to the place of play in early learning and to the development of early childhood pedagogy. We can refer to the work of Robert Owen and James Buchanan, among others, who made attempts to forge a pedagogy away from the dire routine and fear-inducing Dame schools towards making education and coming to school something which children might enjoy. Catherine Isabella Dodd opened an experimental kindergarten which developed such 'new' teaching methods. Maria Montessori, of course, is renowned for her work on using play in a 'controlled environment'; her work was introduced to England by Edward Parnell Culverwell who published *The Montessorian Principles and Practice* in 1913. And John Dewey is perhaps more notable among many who sought to promote a new pedagogy which was more child centred, less prescriptive and not punishment based.

It is Susan Isaacs, though, that we must particularly highlight; her contribution to current understandings of the importance of play cannot be overstated. Her meticulous observations of children making use of a richly stocked environment are still inspiring, and the accounts of teaching and learning in the Malting House School remain central to the archaeology of present-day work on play and the pedagogy of play.

As far back as 1911 and six years after becoming chief inspector for elementary schools in 1905, Edmund Holmes resigned his position and wrote a forceful critique in *What Is and What Might Be: A Study of Education in General and Elementary Education in Particular*. Holmes was alarmed by the prescriptive nature of education in schools at the time and felt it imperative to point out the damaging effect it was having on children and teachers alike. Holmes stated that the real function of education was

> to foster growth. The end which the teacher should set before himself is the development of the latent powers of his pupils, the unfolding of their latent life. If growth is to be fostered, two things must be liberally provided – nourishment and exercise. (Holmes 1911)

Given all that we know of the work and thinking of so many of the pioneers of early childhood education it would be hard to disagree with such things and indeed, Holmes's subsequent writings were taken as an early statement of 'progressive' and 'child-centred' positions. It is therefore not surprising that he was highly critical of those who emphasised education's utilitarian role or as an agent of institutional preservation. Holmes argued that one of the most dangerous aspects of such beliefs was to attach high importance to visible 'results'; the tendency to measure inward worth by outward standards and to judge progress in terms of 'success'. Countering such beliefs, Holmes wrote of

> that deadly system of 'payment by results' which seems to have been devised for the express purpose of arresting growth and strangling life, which bound us all, myself included, with links of iron, and which had many zealous agents, of whom I, alas! was one. (Holmes, 1911)

and that:

> The real 'results' of education are in the child's heart and mind and soul, beyond the reach of any measuring tape or weighing machine. (ibid.)

This seems to be no less of a concern in the pressurised climate of the early twenty-first-century market place where the currency of external appearance is treasured above the value of inward realities; when 'results' seem to matter more than 'quality'. Such trends are no less true for teachers today than they were for Holmes at the beginning of the twentieth century. The rush to succeed and to achieve has too often de-humanised the learning process to the point that teachers can find themselves teaching with an end in sight and pupils passively learning with a result to achieve. The concepts of 'nourishment' and 'exercise' that Holmes espoused become hidden in a system designed to 'deliver the goods', while the deeper, even spiritual, qualities of human beings engaged in learning together are neglected and allowed to waste away.

So is there an antidote to this constant 'ghost' that seems to haunt each generation as it grapples with the changing circumstances of the day? Undoubtedly it is built on the work of Holmes, Dewey, Pestalozzi, Froebel and Comenius, to name but a few, and involves adopting a pedagogy which emphasises learning and play in the early years.

> My children soon became more open, more contented and more susceptible to every good and noble influence than anyone could possibly have foreseen ... I had incomparably less trouble to develop those children whose minds were still blank than those who had already acquired inaccurate ideas ... The children soon felt that there existed in them forces which they did not know ... they acquired a general sentiment of order and beauty ... the impression of weariness which habitually reigns in schools vanished like a shadow from my classroom. They willed, they had power, they persevered, they succeeded, and they were happy. (Pestalozzi 1801: 6)

For Pestalozzi, and so many of the other pioneers, education was important for society as well as for the individual. Education was seen – particularly by Rachel and Margaret McMillan – as a means by which the social regeneration of humanity might be achieved. What these people put forward was a conviction that education is more than just growth for growth's sake but rather growth as a means to a richer quality of life both now and in the future.

5. Early intervention

Current policy and practice in early intervention

The Labour government launched the National Childcare Strategy (NCS) in 1998, a milestone in policy development and a key marker in terms of government investment in early intervention. A central aim of the NCS was to ensure: 'Good quality, affordable childcare for children aged 0 to 14 in every neighbourhood' (DfEE 1998: 5). Issues of work–life balance, and particularly of women contributing to the economy rather than refraining from paid work until their children were over five years old, were main determinants of this policy. This alongside concerns of child protection following high profile cases of abuse, neglect and child killing.

A further strategy was launched in 2004 when *Choice for Parents, the Best Start for Children: A Ten Year Childcare Strategy* (DfES 2004) set out a ten-year strategy. Again, a commitment to support parents in balancing their work life with family needs and child care was central to the national policy. Women, mothers, returning to the workplace was explicit, as was the awareness of the need to address difficulties which were suffered by parents living in socially and economically deprived areas of the country.

In parallel with the 'welfare to work' policy is the government agenda of raising the educational attainment of children and the streamlining and connectedness of services and child protection issues by requiring that local authority services work in an integrated way to provide services for children and families. A longer-term objective was the achievement of better outcomes for children. Never before had there been such a burgeoning weight of policy developments which placed investment commitment to early intervention services and programmes.

Every local authority in England was required to establish multi-agency partnerships (Early Years Development and Childcare Partnerships – EYDCPs) to provide services – with clear emphasis on creating new childcare places, and addressing the need for provision for children under three (hitherto a much neglected area). More recently issues of the quality of provision (Rahilly and Johnston 2002), and the need for a well-trained and appropriately qualified workforce have also been identified as key issues (Abbott and Pugh 1998).

There has been recognition that a 'highly skilled workforce' is central to increasing the number of education and care places and that 'working with children is a demanding, skilled profession' (DfEE 1999: 1). There have been several attempts to develop a single qualifications framework for the education and child care profession but this remains a goal yet to be achieved. Workforce reform builds on recent history in policy and the (then) innovative recommendations of the Rumbold Report (DES 1990), which stressed the importance of highly qualified professionals who could provide what was needed for children and their families. Whatever the policy commitment, until there is adequate funding for further and higher education programmes or a will to address issues of pay for early childhood educators and carers, the policy of high quality early childhood provision will not be fully realised.

As might be expected, such ambitious and rapid policies as have been declared in the last ten years in England also bring controversy. For example, the Early Years Foundation Stage (DfES 2007), introduced in March 2007, listed 69 early learning goals on which children should be assessed when they are five years old. Early years educators continue to try to interpret this framework in a range of home and group settings.

The Sure Start programme began in the UK in 1999, working with a range of agencies in health, employment and education to achieve its comprehensive aims to provide children with a 'sure start' and make them ready to 'flourish'. Working within local communities to develop local projects, the key Sure Start aims are achieved by: helping services develop in disadvantaged areas alongside provision of financial help for parents to afford child care; rolling out the principles driving the Sure Start approach to all services for children and parents. With some variation Sure Start operates in England, Northern Ireland, Scotland and Wales. Investment in Sure Start by 2005–6 amounted to £1.5 billion.

Key elements of the Sure Start programme were:

- *Early education for all*: free part-time early education for three-and four-year-olds in the Foundation Stage.
- *Increased quality and quantity of child care*: start-up grants for childminders, nurseries and after-school care, inspected by the Office for Standards in Education (Ofsted); help for working parents with their childcare costs; local Children's Information Services and a national information service for parents; information for parents and employment advice linked to information on child care.
- *Local programmes*: Children's Centres (with links to Sure Start, Neighbourhood Nurseries and Early Excellence Centres) in the most disadvantaged areas – to offer families early education, childcare and health and family support with advice on employment opportunities.

Sure Start principles   Sure Start supported families from pregnancy until children are 14 years old (16 if they are disabled). The following seven principles underpinned Sure Start work:

1. **Working with parents and children** – Every family should get access to a range of services that will deliver better outcomes for both children and parents, meeting their needs and stretching their aspirations.
2. **Services for everyone** – But not the same service for everyone. Families have distinctly different needs, both between different families, in different locations and across time in the same family. Services should recognise and respond to these varying needs.
3. **Flexible at point of delivery** – All services should be designed to encourage access. For example, opening hours, location, transport issues, and care for other children in the family need to be considered. Where possible we

must enable families to get the health and family support services they need through a single point of contact.

4. **Starting very early** – Services for young children and parents should start at the first antenatal visit. This means not only advice on health in pregnancy, but preparation for parenthood, decisions about returning to work (or indeed, starting work) after the birth, advice on childcare options and on support services available.

5. **Respectful and transparent** – Services should be customer driven, whether or not the service is free.

6. **Community driven and professionally coordinated** – All professionals with an interest in children and families should be sharing expertise and listening to local people on service priorities. This should be done through consultation and by day to day listening to parents.

7. **Outcome driven** – All services for children and parents need to have as their purpose better outcomes for children. The Government needs to acknowledge this by reducing bureaucracy and simplifying funding to ensure a joined up approach with partners.

(Sure Start 2003)

Much Sure Start oriented research has been in the form of evaluation of programmes, and there is a wealth of reports available from the National Evaluation of Sure Start. Hannon (1999) suggested that there are four areas in which educational research can contribute to Sure Start research: *lessons from the past* – drawing on evidence from effective preschool programmes; *relevant research findings* – about, for example, the effects of poverty on early educational attainment; *research into new programmes* – such as those involving parents in early literacy development; and *evaluation methods* – allocating resources for local projects to evaluate their own work through systematic, self-critical and clearly reported evaluation which becomes a means of sharing Sure Start work.

Hannon (ibid.) identified the following questions to ask about Sure Start programmes:

- Are programmes relevant?
- How well is the programme documented?
- For what communities is it designed?
- For what age is it designed?
- Has it been adequately evaluated?
- Is it shown to be valued by families?
- Do claims go beyond evidence?
- Will potential benefits justify resources?
- What staff development implications are there?
- How can the community assess its potential?

Hannon further suggested that local evaluations of Sure Start should consider how they articulate with the national evaluation, their use of external or practitioner research, whether formative or summative, the resources needed and the need for outside support of consultation. Finally, Hannon lists ten points that local evaluations of Sure Start work should cover:

1. Community profile
2. Description of services/implementation
3. Take-up, participation and drop-out
4. Judgements of quality of services
5. Views of staff
6. Views of community
7. Outcomes for children
8. Outcomes for adults
9. Key lessons learned
10. Reporting – sharing – dissemination

(Hannon 1999: 6)

Weinberger *et al.* (2005) report on the collaboration between one local Sure Start programme and its local university over a five-year period to develop and evaluate the initiative. They describe the range of services in health, education and social welfare provided through the Sure Start programme and examine implications for inter-agency work, and lessons learned.

Sure Start programmes are wide ranging and involve a myriad of activities including: family support; work with teenage mothers; breastfeeding support; home safety; smoking cessation; play and learning programmes; language development screening; media literacy projects; reading projects; community involvement. Many are identified through community surveys. Mothers from the Ravensdale area, for example, were surveyed to assess the impact of the Sure Start Breastfeeding Incentive Scheme on their own experiences of breastfeeding their babies. The 26 participants in the survey reported that they valued the midwife support offered and the peer support available from other Sure Start mothers. A total of 23 per cent attributed their continued breastfeeding to the programme (Sharp 2003). In Exeter, a joint nursery and first school developed a 'Ready for School' project to find ways of overcoming social isolation of many children in the area. Initially the project had three elements: a nurture group; a language enrichment programme; and additional support for children's play, language and development. The programme, according to several measures, appeared to make a difference to children's use of language and communication, with many

making better than expected progress. Outcomes included: earlier identification of children with speech and language difficulties; and positive
involvement of parents around their children's learning and development (Randell *et al.* 2004).

Early intervention programmes

The belief that the early years are crucial to children's later educational
achievement, and thus, to their social, emotional and physical development,
has prompted the development of programmes, techniques and strategies
which target young children who are 'at risk' in some way. Early intervention programmes are based on the premise that 'beginning early' means
a greater chance of being successful and are often designed to prevent
difficulties as well as to seek to overcome any difficulties which young
children already have.

Early intervention programmes and strategies are fuelled by the existence
of deep inequalities in many societies and such programmes have to go further than simply providing access to early childhood education or care.
Making it possible to attend some form of preschool provision often misses
the most vulnerable groups, and can fail to provide the necessary support
for children who are vulnerable or at risk of later school failure. The National
Child Development Study (NCDS) began with data from 15,000 children all
born within the same week in the UK in 1958. In the seven-year follow up
it was found that the children's teachers judged far more children whose
parents were unskilled or semi-skilled manual workers to have Special
Educational Needs (24 per cent and 17 per cent) than children whose parents
were in professional groups (4 per cent and 7 per cent) (Davie *et al.* 1972).
The same NCDS sample was studied at age 11 and found that 6 per cent of
the 11-year-olds were 'disadvantaged' – that is, living in single parent or large
families *and* in families with low income *and* poor housing. This 6 per cent were
some three and a half years behind their peers according to reading tests and
more likely to be receiving additional teaching support due to learning difficulties (Wedge and Prosser 1973).

Educational disadvantage is clearly structurally linked to other factors
such as housing, poverty, parent's educational qualifications and so on.
The recent Sure Start programme in the UK can be seen as a large-scale
early intervention programme which seeks to address multiple factors
which threaten children's development. Such programmes seek to provide something specific and additional to usual mainstream provision,
and are often targeted at groups most likely to benefit in an effort to
change something. Many parenting programmes designed to support
parents in managing their toddler's behaviour are early intervention programmes with the aim of bringing about a change in the child's behaviour as a result of the parent changing his or her behaviour.

Since the 1960s there have been several well-known early intervention programmes such as the High Scope Perry Preschool Project (Schweinhart *et al.* 2005, Whitehurst *et al.* 1994). In New Zealand, the 'Reading Recovery' programme was designed to enhance the reading development of children, who, at around six years old, were below their peers in terms of assessed reading attainment. Reading Recovery has since been used in many countries, as a short-term programme whereby children are 'discontinued' and return to usual teaching programmes as soon as they reach an acceptable level of achievement as assessed on a number of tests (Clay 1972).

The crucial issue in relation to early intervention is effectiveness. How can we know that early intervention programmes and strategies will achieve their aims? But such questions require funded studies and can be complex and costly. Bronfenbrenner (1974) reviewed findings of 26 experimental early intervention studies and reported on findings from two types of programme: 'group' and 'parent–child'. Bronfenbrenner's review showed that programmes involving parents had longer-lasting effects than those which only provided or worked with the child. He concluded that programmes which addressed all the factors contributing to educational failure should be developed in the future. It is just this strategy that underpins the Sure Start programmes which seek to support children's learning and development *alongside* strategies to tackle difficulties in families and their communities which militate against healthy progress in childhood.

In the UK there have been few experimental studies which have been designed adequately to evaluate the impact of experimental early intervention programmes. One example of such a study is the 'Raising Achievement in Early Literacy Development' (REAL) project (Nutbrown *et al.* 2005). This study (which took place between 1995 and 2003) brought together the University of Sheffield, the Local Education Authority (LEA) and many Sheffield schools with the aim of promoting family literacy through work with parents of preschool children. From the outset the project had six main aims:

1. To develop methods of working with parents to promote the literacy development of preschool children (particularly those likely to have difficulties in the early years of school).
2. To meet some of the literacy and educational needs of the parents involved.
3. To ensure the *feasibility* of methods developed.
4. To assess the *effectiveness* of the methods in improving children's literacy development at school entry and afterwards.
5. To disseminate effective methods to practitioners and to equip them with new skills.
6. To inform policy-makers about the effectiveness and implications of new practices.

The most promising methods developed in Phase 1 were used to develop an 18-month 'long duration, low intensity' early literacy programme of work with families. Based on the ORIM framework (Nutbrown *et al.* 2005), the programme had five main components: home visits by programme teachers; provision of literacy resources (particularly books); centre-based group activities; special events (for example group library visits); postal communication between teacher and child. The core of the programme was similar at all schools but shaped by local community circumstances and teachers' styles. A total of 80 families from those 10 schools (8 families working with each teacher) participated in the programme. Teachers were funded for release one half day per week to work with the families in their group. Adult learning opportunities for parents were also developed and offered to parents. Outcomes in terms of measures of children's literacy showed that the programme was effective in making a difference to children's literacy, with children in the programme scoring more highly than children in control groups. Nutbrown *et al.* (ibid.) reported that the programme was highly valued by parents who were involved in their children's literacy and by programme teachers who also reported on children's enhanced achievement. Children reported that their parents – mothers *and* fathers – were involved in their home literacy (Nutbrown and Hannon 2003).

Some roots of early intervention

Looking back, we can again see the contribution of the prominent and most eminent of the pioneers. The work of Pestalozzi and his wife demonstrates a commitment to intervene with an effective programme in the life of young children to make a difference to their futures. Maria Montessori, though best known for her method of working with preschool children, began her work by developing a programme to work with nine- and ten-year-old boys who lived on the streets of Rome. Being successful in her work with 'deviant' boys, she revised the programme based on the development and practice of life skills, for use with preschool children.

We cannot forget Robert Owen's contribution to this theme of intervention. His education programme, alongside the whole New Lanark project which included improved sanitation, cooking classes, adult education classes as well as schooling, was designed to intervene in the lives of workers and their families to the better good of the community and of society. It was also, he believed, a way of ensuring a better commitment from his workers and a more wholesome atmosphere in the New Lanark community.

Finally, we cannot leave our discussion on early intervention without mention of Rachel and Margaret McMillan, two women who were committed to improving living conditions for young children, preventing disease and providing play space and nourishment for youngsters from the slums.

What we can see when we look back is that early intervention programmes, often targeted at those with specific needs, have for many centuries been a tool to make a difference in children's lives.

6. Home learning and parents

Current policy and practice in home learning and parental roles in the early years

Research and practice in the past two decades have shed light on parents' roles in their own children's learning and prompted the development of practices and programmes to involve parents more systematically in their own children's education. During the 1960s, programmes to involve parents began to be developed – largely as a way of addressing poor home experiences. However, as it is currently understood the central role of parents in preschool education could perhaps be traced back in policy terms to the Rumbold Report, *Starting with Quality* (DES 1990), which promoted the idea that parents were their children's first and most important educators. Current government policy makes it clear that involvement with parents is an expected part of early childhood education and care in all settings:

> Parents are children's first and most enduring educators. When parents and practitioners work together in early years settings, the results have a positive impact on the child's development and learning. Therefore, each setting should seek to develop an effective partnership with parents. (QCA, DfEE 2000: 9)

There are many examples of parental involvement in children's learning, and, as recent examples have shown (Draper and Duffy 2001; Nutbrown *et al.* 2005; Whalley and the Pen Green Centre Team 2007), the model of parental involvement is largely participative – a far cry from the compensatory ethos which dominated early programmes of the 1960s and 1970s.

Throughout the 1990s, Sheffield LEA, like many others, promoted partnership with parents in schools throughout the city, and 'partnerships' took many forms with workshops, open days, opportunities for adult learning, and special events being offered in many schools across the whole age range from nursery to secondary.

In one school, for example, the 'Parents in Partnership' project led to the development of a programme of accredited learning designed to help parents learn more about their children's learning in order to support them better. An accredited course was designed for the parents, tailored to their needs, with four units: sharing your child's school; sharing your child's reading; sharing your child's maths; sharing your child's science. Parents' comments confirmed the usefulness of the project and the aspirations of many to continue lifelong learning. Some of the comments from parents included:

> I've got a greater awareness of child-centred learning and primary education.
>
> I think that it is easy to sit back and let school and teachers get on with doing their jobs but when I think back to when I was younger and how easy it was not to do any work I want to help my child realise that learning could be fun.
>
> Just being involved helps children because it shows your interest in what they do and helps them to understand it is worthwhile.

> (Firth 1997: 266)

The headteacher of the school at the time reported:

> A key aim is to raise achievement of pupils. Through being involved in the project parents can learn alongside their children and develop better understanding of the expectations of school learning and there is shared understanding of where children's education is coming from and going to. Parents are continuing on their paths of *lifelong* learning too and many have yet to discover where those paths will lead. The potential is tremendous. (ibid.: 267)

Hurst and Joseph (2003) viewed the coming together of parents and practitioners as 'sharing education'. They argued for understanding of the complex cultural differences and shifts which children, parents and practitioners experienced when they entered each other's worlds and examined the opportunities for each to 'share' the other's. However, they concluded that:

> The sharing of intentions and perspectives between parents and practitioners is not easy in a busy classroom. There has to be a rationale for it, and it needs links with a curriculum model which sets a value on children's experiences at home with family and friends. It requires just as much commitment as sharing intentions with children does. Contacts with the home should be seen as a part of the curriculum, and a part of the practitioner's responsibility to provide for children's learning in ways that suit them. The first step is to consider what kind of contact with parents is most valuable, and to find out what kind of contact with the setting is needed by the parents. (Hurst and Joseph 2003: 89)

Specific initiatives to involve parents in the early years have often focused on young children's learning or aspects of curriculum and helping parents learn more about their children's ways of learning. In the late 1980s the 'Froebel Early Learning Project' (Athey 2006) identified ways of helping parents to understand their children's learning interests so that they could better support them. This theme was further developed by Nutbrown (2006) who argued that the more parents know about how children's learning develops, the better position they are in to understand what their children are doing and how they might further enhance learning opportunities for them. More recently the 'PEEP' project in Oxfordshire has developed ways of involving parents with babies and young children in several aspects of their learning and development.

A key issue for research continues to be how to involve parents in ways which are inclusive, participative, respectful and meaningful. Some settings have developed an international reputation for their work in involving parents in their children's learning, for example the Penn Green Centre in Corby (Arnold 2007; Whalley *et al.* 2007), the Coram Children's Centre in London (Draper and Duffy 2001) and the Sheffield Children's Centre. Most recently, Sure Start projects have involved parents in a range of programmes to support them in promoting babies and young children's health, physical, social, emotional and cognitive development. Many settings develop their own specific projects to help parents learn more about their children's learning, such as that reported by Parker (2002) who explains how sharing work with parents on children's drawing and mark making led to enhanced understanding and enthusiasm from parents. Parker records the views of some parents who remarked:

> I have been able to enter her imagination and see the world through her eyes.
>
> Now I'm fascinated by the way she develops a drawing, rather than just looking at the end result.
>
> I have learnt that Brandon is more capable of mark making than I first thought.
>
> (Parker 2002: 92)

Parker notes:

> The parents learned from observing their children and developed an appreciation of their children's high levels of involvement, discussing their children's achievements at home with confidence, clarity and joy … The children have been the primary beneficiaries of this collaboration between parents and practitioners. We all had valuable knowledge and understanding to share. This was a group which enjoyed mutual respect, shared understandings, political awareness and a commitment to extending learning opportunities for young children. (ibid.: 92–3)

In some cases, initiatives have been targeted specifically at minority groups, including families for whom English is not the language of the home. Karran (2003) describes work with parents who are learning English as an additional language and the importance of bilingual support for such parents who want to understand more about education systems and how to help their young children. Siraj-Blatchford (1994) has argued that in some cultures 'education' and 'home' are distinct and separate and time may need to be given to explaining how home–school partnerships can support young children's learning and development. Baz *et al.* (1997) have discussed the importance of bilingual early childhood educators working bilingually with parents and young children using books, early writing, rhymes and poems in families' homes and in group settings.

Some roots of home learning and parental roles in early education

Though it is difficult to identify precise beginnings, parental involvement in their children's learning has, for some time, been part of working with young children. Strong links with the past make the place of the home and family in young children's learning a core and ever-present theme.

In 1803 Pestalozzi's teaching staff wrote six 'Elementary Books', one of which was *The Mother's Manual* or *The Guide to Mothers in Teaching Their Children How to Observe and Think*. In 1900, Edith Mary Deverell joined five other women in the 'Women's Inspectorate' who inspected girls' and elementary schools and made it her goal to promote the interest of parents in their children's education. It is known, furthermore, that around 1915, Margaret McMillan included 'lectures' for parents whose children attended her nursery schools and she was not alone in this strategy to promote parents' knowledge of their children's learning. In 1885, Charlotte Mason was asked by her vicar to make a donation towards St Mark's Anglican Church in Manningham. She did not offer money but suggested that she might give a series of lectures on the education of young children, later published as *Home Education* (Mason 1886). The lectures were attended by a Mrs Francis Steinthal, who, in 1886, helped Mason to form the Parents' Educational Union in Bradford. Charlotte Mason believed strongly in children learning outdoors and learning at home, and remains a key figure in the Home Education movement.

Again, looking back we can see that recent projects to involve parents in their children's learning are not born of new and innovative ideas but are deeply rooted in a view that, as Vygotsky might have said, children's learning is social and the first social group in which children learn is their immediate family.

7. Inclusion

Current policy and practice in inclusion in the early years

The term 'inclusive education' has come to mean many different things which can, in itself, create confusion for students in this area. It is in fact a contestable term used to different effect by politicians, bureaucrats and academics. 'Inclusion' is not a single *movement*; it is made up of many strong currents of belief, many different local struggles and a myriad forms of practices (Clough 2000: 6).

In the UK of the twenty-first century there is increasing demand for inclusive practices and equality of opportunity and access to educational provision. But this has not always been the case and the origins of inclusive education lie in a history of exclusion, segregation and inequality. Clough (2000) traces the roots of inclusion through the last half of the twentieth century (Figure 4.1): from the psycho-medical legacy of the 1950s through the sociological response of the 1960s; curricular approaches which dominated the 1970s; school improvement strategies and programmes of the 1980s; to the disability studies critique and the challenge of the disability movement to the state education system of the 1990s. While acknowledging that this perspective is not the only way of viewing historical developments, Clough suggests that it is these different 'eras' and developments which have led to the current 'era' of inclusion.

It is perhaps because of such recent policy roots that inclusive education is sometimes viewed as the latest term to describe the education of children with Special Educational Needs in mainstream education settings. However, this is not how advocates of inclusive education (or of a broader social inclusion) necessarily define the term. As Booth has it:

> Some continue to want to make inclusion primarily about 'special needs education' or the inclusion in education of children and young people with impairments but that position seems absurd ... If inclusion is about the development of comprehensive community education and about prioritising community over individualism beyond education, then the history of inclusion is the history of these struggles for an education system which serves the interests of communities and which does not exclude anyone within those communities. (Booth 2000: 64)

As provision for education and care for children of all ages considers ways of meeting education targets together with wider social challenges, the 'broad' view of inclusion seems to be gaining currency. Lingard (2000: 101) similarly emphasises the larger structures of inclusion in diversity:

> What I want to do is to hold to a broader definition which links across the whole social justice, equity and citizenship issues. The concept of inclusion might also encourage an across-government approach to social and economic disadvantage.

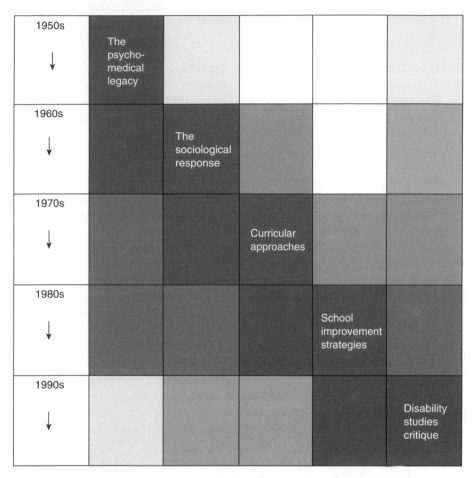

Figure 4.1   A historical interpretation of the development and interaction of ideologies leading to present thinking in inclusive education (Clough 2000: 9)

Barton has argued a major role for inclusive practices in education in order to realise wider changes in society:

> Inclusion is a process. Inclusive education is not merely about providing access into mainstream school for pupils who have previously been excluded. It is not about closing down an unacceptable system of segregated provision and dumping those pupils in an unchanged mainstream system. Existing school systems – in terms of physical factors, curriculum aspects, teaching expectations and styles, leadership roles – will have to change. This is because inclusive education is about the participation of all children and young people and the removal of all forms of exclusionary practice. (Barton 1998: 85)

The development of inclusive education raises many research issues, including:

1. The practicalities of fully inclusive education;
2. Conflicting understandings and definitions of what is meant by 'inclusion';
3. The impact of inclusion and exclusion on the lives of young children;
4. Parents' views and responses to the inclusion and/or exclusion of their children.

Some argue that children with particular needs are difficult to include in mainstream settings and attempts to include children who experience, for example, Emotional and Behavioural Difficulties can be detrimental to some children unless managed with the utmost knowledge and skill (Angelides 2000; Visser *et al.* 2003; Clough *et al.* 2004). Others take the view that there is no justification for the segregation of children in 'Special Schools' because they have a particular impairment (Herbert 1998). Further research is needed to understand the relationship between inclusion and Special Educational Needs and between inclusion and other issues of social justice. Mairian Corker puts it this way:

> I don't like using the term 'special needs' – it's paradoxical to 'inclusion'. I worry that it is increasingly part of a labelling process that is used to pick children off or as a justification for a lack of or a redistribution of resources in a way that is not in the child's interests. These labels are very dehumanising – they really get to the nub of why we are disabled people and not people with disabilities. (Corker 2000: 77)

As Booth (2000) and Lingard (2000) illustrate, definitions of inclusion are contestable. What is meant by 'inclusion' varies from culture to culture, society to society, institution to institution and individual to individual. For example, in some parts of the world (perhaps particularly in the southern hemisphere) the inclusion of indigenous children in education is a key issue in terms of education and social policy and for research (Fleer and Williams-Kennedy 2001). In other parts of the world inclusion of refugee and asylum-seeking families is an issue. Some Traveller families find that they are excluded from educational services or that attempts to include them threaten to violate their cultural heritage and ways of living (Lloyd *et al.* 2003).

The impact of inclusion and exclusion on the lives of young children is a further area for study; we need to know more about the human impact of decisions about young children's early education and care and how pedagogy and learning communities affect their lives and well-being. Parents' views and responses to the inclusion and/or exclusion of their children is a further critical area for research. Berry's (2002) study of four young children's experiences of inclusion demonstrates how important it is that parents have their say in the education of the children they know best and Murray uses poetry and narrative to give voice to parents' experiences of fighting for inclusive inclusion as a right for their children (Murray and Penman 1996).

Inclusive education is as much about helping children to behave inclusively as it is about including particularly marginalised groups of society. Gussin Paley's (1992) work provides one profound example of pedagogy which helps children to include everyone in their play; her well-known book *You Can't Say You Can't Play* documents the development and agreement of this 'rule' for the kindergarten which led to complex understandings and negotiations within an emotionally supportive setting. Gussin Paley's work is not specifically about children with impairment or a particular identified need, but focuses on helping children voice their own stories and demonstrates her pedagogy of inclusion of all children's contributions in the learning setting. The issues of unfairness and discrimination were addressed by Babette Brown in her book *Unlearning Discrimination in the Early Years* (1998), which described how children were supported by their parents and teachers to challenge discrimination and bias:

> Children can become active, enthusiastic and independent learners if, as their educators, we value their cultures and communities, and understand how racism and other social inequalities influence their lives. With our guidance and support children can, as this example illustrates, actively challenge unfairness:
>
>> A group of 6-year-old children were looking through a toy catalogue. They told their teacher that they thought that it wasn't fair because there were no pictures of Black children or any showing girls building or climbing. It was agreed that they should write a letter to the manufacturer. They got no reply so they wrote again. This letter was also unacknowledged. The disappointed children enthusiastically agreed with a parent who suggested that they should draw up a petition. Children, staff and parents signed and it was sent off. To the children's delight the company replied that in future pictures in the catalogue would be more carefully chosen. (ibid.: 3)

The above example shows how children can, with support, challenge exclusive practices and learn strategies to argue for social justice.

The *Index for Inclusion* was first published in 2000 (Booth *et al.* 2000) and issued to all schools in the UK. A second edition was published in 2002 (Booth *et al.* 2002) followed, in 2004, by a specially adapted version for use in early years and childcare settings (Booth and Ainscow 2004). In the words of the introduction, the *Index for Inclusion ... Early Years and Childcare* is:

a resource to support the inclusive development of early years and childcare settings which include: nurseries; playgroups; parent and children centres; crèches; childminding; homecare; clubs and playschemes. The *Index* is a comprehensive document that can help everyone in these settings, to find their own next steps for increasing the participation in play and learning of the children and young people in their care. The materials are designed to build on the knowledge and experience of practitioners and to challenge and support the development of any setting, however 'inclusive' it is thought to be currently (Booth and Ainscow 2004: 1).

In the *Index*, inclusion is an approach to education and child care according to inclusive values, rather than a concern with a particular group of children and young people. Inclusion is often seen to be associated with children and young people who have impairments or are seen as 'having special educational needs'. However, in the *Index* inclusion is concerned with increasing the participation of all children as well as adults: 'We recognise that some children may be more vulnerable to exclusionary pressures than others and argue that settings should become responsive to the diversity of children and young people in their communities' (ibid.).

The *Index* takes a broad definition of inclusion, stressing participation of *all* children and not just the inclusion of a single group (such as children identified as having Special Educational Needs). The *Index* seeks to support practitioners in developing their own responsiveness (and the responsiveness of the systems in place in the setting) to the diversity of children in those learning communities.

Using the *Index* is itself an inclusive activity to ensure that the processes of review, planning for change and putting plans into practice are themselves inclusive. Young children, parents, staff and others associated with the provision are included in the process. All of these aspects of the *Index* provide many avenues for research. Key, of course, is the question as to whether and how using the *Index* makes a difference and how that difference is identified in practice.

The following examples are taken from the *Index for Inclusion* (Booth and Ainscow 2004) and illustrate how people have used the *Index* process to understand more of what young children think about the setting they attend.

Learning to listen

We wanted to find out what our children thought about what we were doing for them. We showed some of our five year olds how to use a digital camera and one at a time, asked them to take pictures of things they liked and things they did not like. One girl came back with a picture of the sensory room [a room where children can control experiences of light, sound and touch]. We were very pleased with that room and so I said 'Oh that's something that you really like?' and she said 'No, I don't like it at all'. She said it 'frightened' her. I learnt my lesson, and was careful, from then on, not to jump to conclusions about what the children thought. We also discussed how we could introduce children to the room so that they could choose the level of interaction with it that they felt comfortable with. (ibid.: 29)

Learning how to consult with parents/carers

The practitioners in a playgroup, serving many families on very low incomes, attempted to consult with parents/carers by handing out an adapted questionnaire. Only those parents/carers who helped out regularly replied. The practitioners invited the others, a few at a time, for a cup of tea after a session, explained the purpose of the questionnaire and talked through the main points. With the parents'/carers' agreement they kept a note of opinions expressed. As a result, the practitioners realised that many parents/carers did not feel involved in the playgroup and did not read the information that was given out. They decided to pair practitioners with parents/carers and encourage them to stay behind for a while after sessions to build relationships and offer support. (ibid.: 31)

The term 'Special Educational Needs' is often used to describe many different physical and learning needs and combinations of needs which have an impact of the form and content of educational provision which is most appropriate for the child. Now widely used, the term came into being in 1978, when the Warnock Report from the Commission on Special Education (DES 1978) concluded that children should not be identified according to 'handicap' and sent to schools which specialised in dealing with that particular 'category' of difficulty, but rather that *educational* difficulties should be identified and provided for accordingly. The term *Special Educational Needs* thus became key in UK education legislation and has been familiar to teachers, other practitioners, parents and policy-makers since that time. *Statements* of Special Educational Need were required to detail the particular needs of children with identified difficulties and an *Individual Education Plan* was developed for each child to detail how their needs would be met in practical terms.

Herbert (1998) suggests that it is difficult to define 'Special Educational Needs' (SEN) in the context of the early years, largely because children with SEN are not a single identifiable group, but individuals with specific and idiosyncratic 'needs'. Children under five wary widely in their growth and development and the years before school are often years of rapid growth and change. Needs change as do the children who are identified as having SEN. Herbert (1998: 94) notes that the 'story' of a child's

Special Educational Needs can often be complex and can involve many agencies and processes including: early identification; medical diagnosis; prediction of need; role of the professionals; inter-agency collaboration; partnership with parents and carers; support and training of staff; the nature of assessment; and differing forms of provision.

The development of provision across the UK during the 1990s, and the drive to provide for all young children where there is specific need and all three- and four-year-olds whose parents wish them to attend some form of provision, has highlighted the need to identify and support children whose needs are particular or who fall into what is termed *Special Educational Needs*. SEN has become an issue for the majority of settings and is a concern of all practitioners – to varying degrees – from time to time. Roffey (2001) highlights the importance of collaboration, communication and co-ordination between agencies and between providers, practitioners and families. *Special Educational Needs* is no longer an issue only for *Special* Schools but it is likely that most early years settings will provide for some children who are identified as having *SEN*.

The 2001 *Code of Practice on the Identification and Assessment of Special Educational Needs* (DfES 2001) marked a shift in thinking in relation to SEN which will carry important implications for providing for children with SEN. According to the Code of Practice there are four principal areas of special educational need, which relate to:

1. Communication and interaction
2. Cognition and learning
3. Behaviour, emotional and social development
4. Sensory and/or physical impairment.

The Code stated that a child has Special Educational Needs if s/he has a learning difficulty which necessitates *special educational provision*. Their difficulties may be apparent if:

- a child has a significantly greater difficulty in learning than the majority of children of the same age;
- a child has a disability which prevents or hinders him/her from making use of educational facilities of a kind generally provided for children of the same age in schools within the area of the local education authority
- a child is under five years of age and falls within either definition above or would do so if special education provision was not made for the child.

(Clough and Garner 2003)

Early education settings have, for many years, given priority to children with learning difficulties or to those identified as having SEN, and

Nutbrown (1998) has argued that early education – at its best – is *inclusive education* because of the emphasis, in practice, on identifying and meeting the individual learning needs of all young children. It is often the experience of those who work in early years settings that young children are included as a first option. Many such settings would argue that supporting children with learning difficulties is as much about an *attitudinal* response as it is about *practical* responses.

Research in recent years has begun to focus on telling the stories of children within the SEN category, and of how they fare in Special and Mainstream Schools (Berry 2002; Pereera 2000; Wise and Glass 2000), but more such accounts are needed, in order to help practitioners and policy-makers learn more of the experiences of parents, children and practitioners so involved.

Studies are also needed of the relationship between addressing learning difficulties, meeting Special Educational Needs, inclusive education and how learning difficulties are variously 'constructed' by parents, policy-makers and practitioners. There are often diverse views on what 'Special Educational Needs' are, and on how they should be met. Many such views are inferred from particular sets of circumstances and, Clough argues, give rise to the following questions which could well form part of a research agenda:

- Where do the various 'constructions' of difficulty come from?
- How are they evidenced?
- How are they communicated?
- How are they challenged? How do they change?
- Who changes constructions of educational need, of difference and of difficulty? (2000: 6)

In 1971, Italy was one of the first countries in Europe to legislate for the integration of children with learning difficulties into mainstream schooling. In 1997 the law stated that: 'All children with handicaps, regardless of the nature and seriousness of their handicaps, are to be integrated in normal mainstream school classes' (Menegoi-Buzzi 1999: 18). In the Reggio Emilia preschools of Northern Italy, children with learning difficulties are regarded as having *Special Rights* (rather than Special Needs) and Phillips (2001) argues that the Reggio *pedagogy of listening* gives 'voice' to all young children in Reggio preschools.

Some roots of inclusion

In recent years, in the UK, there has been massive expansion of provision for children under five and, in many cases, children whose families live in areas of deprivation have been targeted to receive additional help through government initiatives such as Sure Start, and support for children with learning difficulties is often now a matter of priority.

If we try to find the roots of inclusive education, we find specific groups are often identified as in need of provision. Pestalozzi did not only provide education for abandoned children, but also made a point of providing schooling for girls. Rousseau, though focusing on the education of boys in particular, set out the principles of educating girls as well. Something which others, including Charlotte Mason, the McMillan sisters and Sir John Newsom were also committed to.

Mary Humphrey, in 1890, began what might be seen as an early Sure Start programme, providing play hours, a social centre (and bible teaching). She later set up a similar scheme for what she called 'crippled' children, paving the way for some recognition of the need for additional programmes of support for children with Special Educational Needs.

The education of 'the poor' was a focus for Joshua Watson who founded the National Society for the Education of the Poor in the Principles of the Established Church in 1811. The McMillan sisters, in the early 1900s, developed nursery schools for the children of the poor and succeeded in developing provision that addressed children's health issues which inhibited their growth and development.

Though not carried out under the banner of 'Inclusion', the driving force of the work of these pioneers was one of promoting social justice and combating exclusive practices which marginalised and inhibited the development of specific groups of society. This is a set of values which would be recognised by many who advocate inclusive education and the development of an inclusive society in the twenty-first century.

Conclusion

An overarching theme which brings together the seven issues and their histories which we discussed in the final part of the book is that of training. Whenever a need was identified or specific programmes and initiatives developed, the need to train others to be able also to do the work was identified and addressed. This is all but explicit in the case of every one of the pioneers discussed in this book. This was not simply a solution to a practice problem of needing others to do the work they had pioneered, but a deep recognition that no one can stand alone. And in their commitment to training for teachers, these pioneers were committed to passing on their knowledge to others and thus giving others the tools with which to do their job. It also makes it clear how, even though we have drawn on the names and particular works of a small number of people, behind them and around them were countless hundreds of other partners and apprentices involved in developing and improving practice and provision for young children. None of them was an 'island' and their biographies testify to collaboration and co-operation. For those who work in the twenty-first century on issues which others identified and sought to address in the past, collaboration and partnership remains essential so that, brick by brick, the work gets done.

What is education for?

This question of what education is 'for' must have been in the minds of many of the figures from history whom we have featured in this book. There must have been a profound belief in the capacity of education to bring about change.

In essence, education is for the individual; learning is first and foremost for the learner. Politicians may talk of education being the means by which society can be improved, opportunities increased and the economy boosted – as if such things were *the prime reason for learning*. To be sure, society and the economy of a country are enhanced as a result of improved education, but education is about something else as well, and should be valued as a way of helping individual men, women and children to become more fully aware of themselves and their potential within themselves to develop as human beings. During the 1980s the Latin word '*educare*' (to lead forth) became a popular term to describe early childhood settings. We can apply the meaning of *educare* to all education, where we see everyone as having a personal 'reservoir of potential' from which they can draw – that is education.

What is *early* education for?

So what, then, is *early* education for? For us, in the spirit of Vygotsky's theory of learning, learning is about relationships, and in the early years relationships are key. This is why the development of the 'Key Person' (Rouse-Selleck, Goldschmeid and Elfer, 2003) in work with babies and toddlers is so crucial, and also why the central role of the parent in a child's development and learning is vital, much as Mason described. Young children are full of drive to discover the potential within themselves and the world around them and relationships support discovery.

In this book we have looked back at the work of the past and examined present policies, practice and research in order to understand better what is happening now and to be equipped with an improved understanding of ideas which may come in the future. It was in 1953 that L. P. Hartley wrote in *The Go-Between*, 'The past is a foreign country; they do things differently there.' The past may well be a foreign country, but as we know, travellers to other countries often learn something new, collect an interesting artefact, a different recipe, a new idea, bring something back which changes their lives, even just a little. Look at the past and we see our present, and perhaps our future through new lenses ... and as Comenius wrote in the 1600s:

> We are all citizens of one world, we are all of one blood. To hate a man because he was born in another country, because he speaks a different language, or because he takes a different view on this subject or that, is a great folly. Desist, I implore you, for we are all equally human ... Let us have but one end in view, the welfare of humanity; and let us put aside all selfishness in considerations of language, nationality, or religion. (Comenius 1657)

Different views and practices may be foreign to us, but understanding how they came to be puts us in a position to understand, or to challenge.

As we have written this book we have found ourselves saying, 'What would Susan Isaacs say about that?' or 'How would Pestalozzi have responded to this?' But we want to align ourselves with Christian Schiller and, in paying tribute to and learning from the work that others before us have done, go forward and make our way 'into the future':

> there have been great men and women whose vision and action have inspired a generation: Robert Owen, Friedrich Froebel, in our own time Margaret McMillan and others. But they pass away, and their ideas pass away with them unless these

ideas are fashioned into new forms which reflect new circumstances and stand the test of new practices in the contemporary scene. The pioneers take such ideas and refashion and temper them in their daily work in school. Patiently, day after day, week after week and year after year they make the pathway from the past through the present towards the future. (Schiller 1951: xvii)

The important thing in early childhood education is not what Susan Isaacs, or Charlotte Mason, or Katherine Bathurst might have said. The important thing is what those who live with, or work with and for young children in our present times and settings say and do. The important thing is that the new pioneers, those working in early childhood settings and elsewhere in the pursuit of the best provision for young children, take these ideas into the future and make them their own. There is no better tribute to those who have gone than to remould, revisit and revise their ideas for a new today.

So who needs history?

We suggest that we need to understand the history of early childhood education because it provides a 'rootedness' to our work. It means we are building our work on solid ground and travelling along well-trodden paths. We can be inspired by some whose ideas came – as it were – before their time but yet were not reticent in articulating or realising their ideas. History can remind us that it is worth working for the things you believe in and the study of history shows how important it is to record ideas and practices for those who follow to ponder.

Do not dwell in the past, do not dream of the future, concentrate the mind on the present moment.

Siddhartha Buddha (C. 563 BC – 483 BC)

References, further reading, historical archives and other sources consulted

Abbott, L. and Pugh, G. (1998) *Training to work in the early years: developing the climbing frame*. Buckingham: Open University Press.

Aeppli, W. (1986) *Rudolf Steiner Education and the Developing Child*. Hudson, NY: Anthroposophic Press.

Alderson, P. (2000) *Young Children's Rights: Exploring Beliefs, Principles and Practice*. London: Jessica Kingsley Publishers.

Aldrich, R. and Gordon, P. (1989) *Dictionary of British Educationists*. London: The Woburn Press.

Angelides, P. (2000) 'A new technique for dealing with behaviour difficulties in Cyprus: the analysis of critical incidents', *European Journal of Special Needs Education* 15(1), 55–68.

Anning, A. and Edwards, A. (2003) 'Language and literacy learning', in J. Devereaux and L. Miller (eds), *Working with Children in the Early Years*. London: David Fulton Publishers/Open University.

Arnold, C. (2007) 'Persistence pays off: working with "hard to reach" parents', in M. Whalley and the Pen Green Centre Team, *Involving Parents in their Children's Learning* (2nd edn). London: Paul Chapman Publishing.

Athey, C. (2006) *Extending Thought in Young Children: A Parent–Teacher Partnership* (2nd edn). London: Paul Chapman Publishing.

Backstrom, K. (1997) 'The significance of the UN Convention on the Rights of the Child to children in preschool and school'. Paper given at the 22nd International Montessori Congress, 'The Child and Communication', 22–27 July 1997. Available online at: http://www.ilu.uu.se/ilu/montessori/index/htm

Baghban, M. (1984) *Our Daughter Learns to Read and Write*. Delaware, NY: International Reading Association.

Baker, S. and Freeman, D. (2005) *The Love of God in the Classroom: The Story of the New Christian Schools*. Rosshire, Scotland: Christian Focus.

Barton, L. (1998) *The Politics of Special Educational Needs*. Lewes: Falmer Press.

Baz, P., Begun, L., Chia, K., Mason, G., Nutbrown, C. and Wragg, L. (1997) 'Working bilingually with families', in C. Nutbrown and P. Hannon (eds), *Preparing for Early Literacy Education with Parents*: *A Professional Development Manual*. Nottingham/Sheffield: NES Arnold/University of Sheffield, School of Education.

Bennett, N. and Kell, J. (1989) *A Good Start? Four Year Olds in Infant Schools*. Oxford: Blackwell.

Bennett, N., Wood, E. and Rogers, S. (1997) *Teaching through Play: Teachers' Thinking and Classroom Practice*. Buckingham: Open University Press.

BERA EYSIG (British Educational Research Association Early Years Special Interest Group) (2003) *Early Years Research: Pedagogy, Curriculum and Adult Roles, Training and Professionalism*. Nottingham: BERA.

Berry, T. (2002) 'Does inclusion work? Simon's story', in C. Nutbrown (ed.), *Research Studies in Early Childhood Education*. Stoke-on Trent: Trentham Books.

Bertram, C. (2003) *Rousseau and 'The Social Contract'*. London: Routledge.

Bettlelheim, B. (1982) *Freud and Man's Soul*. New York: Knopf.

Bettlelheim, B. (1988) *The Uses of Enchantment: The Meaning and Importance of Fairy Tales*. Harmondsworth: Penguin.

Biber, G. E. (1831) *Henry Pestalozzi and his Plan of Education*. London: John Souter, School Library.

Bissex, G. L. (1980) *GYNS AT WRK: A Child Learns to Write and Read*. Cambridge, MA: Harvard University Press.

Board of Education (1936) *Nursery Schools and Nursery Classes*. Education Pamphlet, No. 106. London: HMSO, pp. 39–53.

Booker, S. (1995) *'We are your children': the Kushanda Early Childhood Education and Care Dissemination Programme. Zimbabwe 1985–93* (extracts). Early Childhood Development: Practice and Reflections, Number 7, Bernard Van Leer Foundation.

Booth, T. (2000) 'Reflection: Tony Booth', in P. Clough and J. Corbett (2000) *Theories of Inclusive Education*. London: Paul Chapman Publishing.

Booth, T. and Ainscow, M. (2004) *Index for Inclusion: Developing Learning, Participation and Play in Early Years and Childcare*. Bristol: Centre for Studies in Inclusive Education. The *Index* is available from: CSIE, 1 Redland Close, Elm Lane, Redland, Bristol BS6 6UE.

Booth, T., Ainscow, M., Black-Hawkins, K., Vaughan, M. and Shaw, L. (2000) *Index for Inclusion: Developing Learning and Participation in Schools*. Bristol: Centre for Studies in Inclusive Education.

Booth, T., Ainscow, M., Black-Hawkins, K., Vaughan, M. and Shaw, L. (2002) *Index for Inclusion: Developing Learning and Participation in Schools* (2nd edn). Bristol: Centre for Studies in Inclusive Education.

Bredekamp, S. (ed.) (1987) *Developmentally Appropriate Practice in Early Childhood Programs Serving Children from Birth through Age 8*, expanded edn. Washington, DC: NAEYC.

Bronfenbrenner, U. (1974) *A Report on Longitudinal Evaluations of Preschool Programs. Vol 2: Is Early Intervention Effective?* Washington, DC: DHEW.

Brown, B. (1998) *Unlearning Discrimination in the Early Years*. Stoke-on-Trent: Trentham Books.

Burke, C. (1982) 'Redefining written language growth: the child as informant'. Paper presented at the 8th Australian Reading Association Conference, Adelaide.

Cholmondeley, E. (1960)*The Story of Charlotte Mason 1842–1923*. London: Dent.

Chomsky, N. (1993) *Language and Thought*. Wakefield, RI and London: Moyer Bell.

Christmas, J. (2005) 'Is it OK to play?', in K. Horst, and C. Nutbrown (eds), *Perspectives on Early Education: Essays in Contemporary Research*. Stoke-on-Trent: Trentham Books.

City of Edinburgh Council/Early Education (1999) *Excellence from the Start: Edinburgh Nursery Schools from 1903 to the Present Day*. CD-ROM. For details contact Moira Small, BAECE, 19 Dalhousie Terrace, Edinburgh, EH10 5NE.

Clay, M. (1972) *Reading Recovery: The Patterning of Complex Behaviour*. Auckland: Heinemann.

Cleave, S. and Brown, S. (1991) *Early to School: Four Year Olds in Infant Classes.* Slough: NFER/Nelson.

Clegg, A. (1980) *About Our Schools.* London: Blackwell.

Clough, P. (ed.) (1998) *Managing Inclusive Education: From Policy to Experience.* London: Paul Chapman Publishing.

Clough, P. (2000) 'Routes to inclusion', in P. Clough and J. Corbett, *Theories of Inclusive Education.* London: Paul Chapman Publishing.

Clough, P. and Corbett, J. (2000) *Theories of Inclusive Education.* London: Paul Chapman Publishing.

Clough, P. and Garner, P. (2003) 'Special educational needs and inclusive education: origins and current issues', in S. Bartlett and D. Burton (eds), *Education Studies: Essential Issues.* London: Sage.

Clough, P., Garner, P., Pardeck, J. T. and Yuen, F. (eds) (2004) *Handbook of Emotional and Behavioural Difficulties.* London: Sage.

Clough, P. and Nutbrown, C. (2002) 'The Index for Inclusion: personal perspectives from early years educators', *Early Education* 26 (Spring).

Clough, P. and Nutbrown, C. (2003) 'The "Index for Inclusion": perspectives of early years practitioners', in M. Nind, K. Sheehy and K. Simmons (eds), *Inclusive Education: Learners and Learning Contexts.* London: David Fulton Publishers.

Clough, P. and Nutbrown, C. (2004) 'Special Educational Needs and Inclusive early education: multiple perspectives from UK educators', *Journal of Early Childhood Research* 2(2), 191–211.

Cohen, D. (1997) *Carl Rogers: A Critical Biography.* London: Constable.

Cole, M. (1997) 'Equality and primary education: what are the conceptual issues?', in M. Cole, D. Hill and S. Shan, *Promoting Equality in Primary Schools.* London: Cassell, pp. 48–75.

Coles, R. (1970) *Erik H. Erikson: The Growth of His Work.* Boston, MA and Toronto: Little, Brown.

Collins, P. (1963) *Dickens and Education.* London: Macmillan.

Comenius, J. A. (1923) *The Great Didactic of John Amos Comenius* [1657]. Translated into English and edited with biographical, historical and critical introductions by M. W. Keatinge. London: A. & C. Black.

Comenius, J. A. (1956) *The School of Infancy* [1631], edited with an introduction by E. M. Eller. Chapel Hill, NC: University of North Carolina Press.

Comenius, J. A. (1968) *Orbis Sensualium Pictus: A Facsimile of the First English Edition of 1659* [1658]. Introduced by J. E. Sadler. London: Oxford University Press.

Comenius, J. A. (1986) *Comenius's Pampaedia or Universal Education,* ed. and trans. A. M. O. Dobble. Dover: Buckland.

Connolly, P. (2004) *Boys and Schooling in the Early Years.* London: RoutledgeFalmer.

Cooper, L. (1999) *Rousseau, Nature and the Problem of the Good Life.* University Park, PA: Pennsylvania State University Press.

Cordes, C. and Millar, E. (2000) *Fools Gold: A Critical look at Computers in Childhood.* College Park, MD: Alliance for Childhood.

Corker, M. (2000) 'Profile: Mairian Corker', in P. Clough and J. Corbett (2000) *Theories of Inclusive Education.* London: Paul Chapman Publishing.

Covell, K. and Howe, R. B. (1999) *Children's Rights Education Curriculum Resource.* Cape Breton, Nova Scotia: University College of Cape Breton Children's Rights Centre.

Cranston, M. (1982) *Jean-Jacques: The Early Life and Work.* New York: Norton.

Croall, J. (1983) *Neill of Summerhill: The Permanent Rebel*. London: Routledge and Kegan Paul.

Culverwell, E. P. (1913) *The Montessorian Principles and Practice*. London: G. Bell and Sons.

Damrosch, L. (2005) *Jean-Jacques Rousseau: Restless Genius*. New York: Houghton Mifflin.

David, T. and Powell, S. (1999) 'Changing childhoods, changing minds', in T. David (ed.), *Young Children Learning*. London: Paul Chapman Publishing.

Davie, R., Butler, N. and Goldstein, H. (1972) *From Birth to Seven: A Report of the National Child Development Study*. London: Longman.

Dent, N. J. H. (1988) *Rousseau: An Introduction to his Psychological, Social, and Political Theory*. Oxford: Blackwell.

Dent, N. J. H. (2005) *Rousseau*. London: Routledge.

DES (Department of Education and Science) (1978) *Special Educational Needs: Report of the Committee of Inquiry into the Education of Handicapped Children and Young People*. The Warnock Report. London: HMSO.

DES (Department of Education and Science) (1988) *English for Ages 5–11: Proposals of the Secretary of State for Education and Science and the Secretary of State for Wales*. London: National Curriculum Council.

DES (Department of Education and Science) (1990) *Starting with Quality: Report of the Committee of Inquiry into the Quality of Educational Expereince Offered to Three and Four Year Olds*. The Rumbold Report. London: HMSO.

Dewey, J. (1897) *Experience and Education*. New York: Macmillan Publishing Co.

Dewey, J. (1897) *How We Think*. New York: Dover Publications.

Dewey, J. (1897) *My Pedagogic Creed*. Washington, DC: Progressive Education Association.

Dewey, J. (1899) *The School and Society*. Chicago, IL: University of Chicago Press.

Dewey, J. (1931) *The Way Out of Educational Confusion*. Cambridge, MA: Harvard University Press.

DfEE (Department for Education and Employment) (1997) *Excellence in Schools*. London: The Stationery Office.

DfEE (Department for Education Employment) (1998) 'Developing a more inclusive education system', in *Meeting Special Educational Needs: A Programme for Action*. Sudbury: DfEE Publications Centre.

DfEE (Department for Education and Employment) (1999) *Sure Start: Making a Difference for Children and Families*. London: DfEE.

DfES (Department for Education and Skills) (2001) *Code of Practice on the Identification and Assessment of Children with Special Educational Needs*. London: HMSO.

DfES (Department for Education and Skills) (2004) *Choice for Parents, the Best Start for Children: A Ten Year Childcare Strategy*. London: DfES.

DfES (Department for Education and Skills) (2005) *Every Child Matters: Change for Children*. London: HMSO.

DfES (Department for Education and Skills) (2007) *Statutory Framework for the Early Years Foundation Stage: Setting the Standards for Learning, Development and Care for Children from Birth to Five*. London: HMSO.

DfES (Department for Education and Skills)/QCA (Qualifications and Curriculum Authority) (2003) *Foundation Stage Profile Handbook*. London: QCA.

Dickens, C. (1994) *Great Expectations* [1861]. Harmondsworth: Penguin.

Dickens, C. (1999) *Nicholas Nickleby* [1839]. Harmondsworth: Penguin.

Dickens, C. (2003) *Bleak House* [1852]. Harmondsworth: Penguin.

Dickens, C. (2004) *David Copperfield* [1850]. Harmondsworth: Penguin.

Dickens, C. (2007) *Hard Times* [1854]. Harmondsworth: Penguin.

Donaldson, M. (1986) *Children's Minds*. London: Fontana.

Draper, L. and Duffy, B. (2001) 'Working with parents', in G. Pugh (ed.), *Contemporary Issues in the Early Years: Working Collaboratively for Children*. London: Paul Chapman Publishing.

Dyson, A. H. (1997) *Writing Superheroes: Contemporary Childhood, Popular Culture and Classroom Literacy*. New York: Teachers College Press.

Dyson, A. H. (2002) *Brothers and Sisters Learn to Write Popular Literacies in Childhood and School Cultures*. New York: Teachers College Press.

Erikson, E. (1950) *Childhood and Society*. New York: W. W. Norton.

Erikson, E. (1958) *Young Man Luther: A Study in Psychoanalysis and History*. New York: W. W. Norton.

Erikson, E. (1963) *Youth: Change and Challenge*. New York: Basic Books.

Erikson, E. (1964) *Insight and Responsibility*. New York: W. W. Norton.

Erikson, E. (1968) *Identity: Youth and Crisis*. New York: W. W. Norton.

Feldman, M. (ed.) (2004) *Early Intervention: The Essential Readings*. Oxford: Blackwell.

Ferrerio, E. and Teberosky, A. (1989) *Literacy before Schooling*. Oxford: Heinemann.

Firth, R. (1997) 'Brunswick Primary School "Parents in Partnership" Project', in C. Nutbrown and P. Hannon (eds), *Preparing for Early Literacy Education with Parents: A Professional Development Manual*. Nottingham/Sheffield: NES Arnold/University of Sheffield, School of Education.

Fleer, M. and Williams-Kennedy, D. (2001) *Building Bridges: Literacy Development in Young Indigenous Children*. Canberra: Department of Education, Science and Training.

Freire, P. (1972) *Pedagogy of the Oppressed*. London: Penguin.

Freud, S. (1917). *A Childhood Recollection* [from Dichtung Und Wahrheit]. *The Standard Edition of the Complete Psychological Works of Sigmund Freud, Volume XVII (1917–1919): An Infantile Neurosis and Other Works*, 145–156.

Freud, S. (1953–64) *The Standard Edition of the Complete Psychological Works of Sigmund Freud*, 24 vols, ed. J. Stratchey with A. Freud. London: Hogarth Press.

Friedman, L. J. (1999) *Identity's Architect: A Biography of Erik H. Erikson*. New York: Charles Scribner.

Froebel, F. (1826) *The Education of Man* (*Die Menschenerziehung*). Keilhan/Leipzig: Wienbranch.

Froebel, F. (1843) *Mother Songs* (*Mutter und Koselieder*). Keilhan/Leipzig: Wienbranch.

Frosh, S. (1987) *The Politics of Psychoanalysis: An Introduction to Freudian and Post-Freudian Theory*. London and New Haven, CT: Yale University Press.

Fulghum, R. (1989) *All I Really Need to Know I Learned in Kindergarten: Uncommon Thoughts on Common Things*. New York: Ivy Books.

Gardner, D. E. M. (1969) *Susan Isaacs*. London: Routledge and Kegan Paul.

Gattico, E. (2001) *Jean Piaget*. Milan: Bruno Mondadori.

Gillespie, A. (2006) 'Children, art and artists', *Early Education* (Summer), 3–7.

Goldson, B. (1997) '"Childhood": an introduction to historical and theoretical analyses', in P. Scraton (ed.), *'Childhood' in 'Crisis'?* London: UCL Press.

Goodman, K. (1967) 'Reading: a psycholinguistic guessing game', *Journal of the Reading Specialist* 6, 126–35.

Goodman, K., Goodman, Y. and Burke, C. (1978) 'Reading for life – the psycholinguistic base', in E. Hunter-Grundin and H. U. Hunter-Grundin (eds), *Reading: Implementing the Bullock Report.* London: Ward Lock.

Goodman, Y. (1980) 'The roots of literacy', in M. P. Douglass (ed.), *Claremont Reading Conference 44th* Yearbook. Claremont, CA: Claremont Reading Conference, pp. 1–32.

Goodman, Y. (1986) 'Children coming to know literacy', in W. H. Teale and E. Sulzby (eds), *Emergent Literacy Writing and Reading.* Norwood, NJ: Ablex Publishing Corporation.

Goswami, U. and Bryant, P. (1990) *Phonological Skills and Learning to Read.* Hove: Lawrence Erlbaum Associates.

Grunelius, E. von (1974) *Educating the Young Child.* London: New Knowledge Books.

Gussin Paley, V. (1992) *You Can't Say You Can't Play.* Cambridge, MA: Harvard University Press.

Hancock, R. and Cox, A. (2002) '"I would have worried about her being a nuisance": workshops for children under three and their parents at Tate Britain', *Early Years* 22(2), 118.

Hannon, P. (1980) 'Preschool care and education: historical and psychological issues with implications for policy', Working Paper. Sheffield: University of Sheffield, Division of Education.

Hannon, P. (1999) *What Can Educational Research Offer Sure Start?* Briefing note commissioned by the NHS Executive (Trent Region) for a symposium held in Derby, 29 March 1999. Sheffield: University of Sheffield, Department of Educational Studies.

Hannon, P., Morgan, A. and Nutbrown, C. (2006) 'Parents' experiences of a family literacy programme', *Journal of Early Childhood Research* 3(3), 19–44.

Hardy, L. (1919) *The Diary of a Free Kindergarten* [1912]. Edinburgh: The City of Edinburgh/Early Education.

Harrett, J. (2001) 'Young children talking: an investigation into the personal stories of Key Stage One infants', *Early Years* 22(1), 19–26.

Harste, J. C., Woodward, V. A. and Burke, C. L. (1984) *Language Stories and Literacy Lessons.* Portsmouth, N. H: Heinemann Educational Books.

Herbert, E. (1998) 'Included from the start? Managing early years settings for all', in P. Clough (ed.), *Managing Inclusive Education: From Policy to Experience.* London: Paul Chapman Publishing.

Hesse, H. (1976) *My Belief: Essays on Life and Art.* NY: Farrar, Straus and Giroux.

Hickson, H. (2003) 'Developing the role of parents in early writing experiences of their children', in *Summaries of Action Research Reports.* Tameside LEA/University of Sheffield, School of Education.

Hiebert, E. H. (1981) 'Developmental patterns and inter-relationships of preschool children's print awareness', *Reading Research Quarterly* 16, 236–59.

Hirst, K. (1998) 'Pre-school literacy experiences of children in Punjabi, Urdu and Gujarati speaking families in England', *British Educational Research Journal* 24(4), 415–29.

HMI (Her Majesty's Inspectors of Schools) (1989) *The Education of Children Under Five: Aspects of Education Series*. London: Department of Education and Science, pp. 5–19.

Holland, P. (2003) *We Don't Play with Guns Here*. Buckingham: Open University Press.

Holmes, E. G. A. (1911) *What Is and What Might Be: A Study of Education in General and Elementary Education in Particular*. London: Coustable.

Holt, J. (1990) *How Children Fail*. Harmondsworth: Penguin.

Hughes, J. L. (1900) *Dickens as an Educator*. New York: D. Appleton.

Hutt, S. J., Tyler, S., Hutt, C. and Christopherson, H. (1989) *Play, Exploration and Learning: A Natural History of the Preschool*. London: Routledge.

Hurst, V. And Joseph, J. (2003) *Supporting Early Learning – the Way Forward: The Way Forward*. Buckingham: Open University Press.

Hyder, T. (2004) *War, Conflict and Play*. Buckingham: Open University Press.

Inkpen, M. (1996) *Nothing*. London: Hodder and Stoughton.

Isaacs, S. S. (1954) *The Educational Value of the Nursery School*. London: The Nursery Schools Association of Great Britain and Northern Ireland.

Isaacs, S. S. (1929) *The Nursery Years*. London: Routledge and Kegan Paul.

Isaacs, S. S. (1930) *Intellectual Growth in Young Children*. London: Routledge and Kegan Paul.

Isaacs, S. S. (1933) *Social Development of Young Children*. London: Routledge and Kegan Paul.

Jenkinson, S. (2001) *The Genius of Play: Celebrating the Spirit of Childhood*. Stroud: Hawthorn Press.

Jones, E. (1953–57) *Sigmund Freud: Life and Work* 3 vols, New York: Basic Books.

Karran, S. (2003) '"Auntie-Ji, please come and join us, just for an hour": the role of the bilingual education assistant in working with parents with little confidence', in J. Devereaux and L. Miller (eds), *Working with Children in the Early Years*. London: David Fulton Publishers/Open University Press.

Kelly, T. (1970) *A History of Adult Education in Great Britain*. Liverpool: Liverpool University Press.

Kenway, M. and Bullen, E. (2001) *Consuming Children: Education – Entertainment – Advertising*. Buckingham: Open University Press.

Kilpatrick, W. H. (1916) *Froebel's Kindergarten Principles Critically Examined*. New York: Macmillan.

Kirschenbaum, H. (1979) *On Becoming Carl Rogers*. New York: Delacorte Press.

Kitchener, R. (1986) *Piaget's Theory of Knowledge*. New Haven, CT: Yale University Press.

Kramer, R. (1976) *Maria Montessori*. Toronto: Longman Canada Limited.

Kraut, R. (1984) *Socrates and the State*. Princeton, NJ: Princeton University Press.

Lange, L. (2002) *Feminist Interpretations of Jean-Jacques Rousseau*. University Park, PA: Pennsylvania State University Press.

Laurie, S. S. (1904) *John Amos Comenius, Bishop of Moravians: His Life and Educational Works* (6th edn). Cambridge: Cambridge University Press.

Lawrence, E. (ed.) (1952) *Friedrich Froebel and English Education*. London: University of London Press.

Lindqvist, G. (2001) 'When small children play: how adults dramatise and children create meaning', *Early Years* 21(1), 7–14.

Lingard, B. (2000) 'Profile: Bob Lingard', in P. Clough and J. Corbett (2000) *Theories of Inclusive Education*. London: Paul Chapman Publishing.

Lissau, R. (1987) *Rudolf Steiner: Life, Work, Inner Path and Social Initiatives*. Stroud: Hawthorn Press.

Lloyd, G., Stead, J., Jordan, E. and Norris, C. (2003) 'Teachers and Gypsy Travellers', in M. Nind, K. Sheehy and K. Simmons (eds), *Inclusive Education: Learners and Learning Contexts*. London: David Fulton Publishers.

Lowenfeld, M. (1935) *Play in Childhood*. London: Gollanz.

McBratney, S. (1994) *Guess How Much I Love You*. London: Walker Books.

Maclean, M., Bryant, P. and Bradley, L. (1987) 'Rhymes, nursery rhymes and reading in early childhood', *Merrill-Palmer Quarterly* 33(3), 255–81.

McMillan, M. (1896) *Child Labour and the Half Time System*. London: George Allen and Unwin.

McMillan, M. (1900) *Early Childhood*. London: George Allen and Unwin.

McMillan, M. (1917) *The Camp School*. London: George Allen and Unwin.

McMillan, M. (1919) *The Nursery School*. London: George Allen and Unwin.

McMillan, M. (1920) *Nursery Schools: A Practical Handbook*. London: George Allen and Unwin.

McMillan, M. (1925) *Childhood, Culture, and Class in Britain*. London: George Allen and Unwin.

McMillan, M. (1927) *The Life of Rachel McMillan*. London: J. M. Dent.

Malaguzzi, L. (1996) 'The right to environment', in T. Filippini and V. Vecchi (eds), *The Hundred Languages of Children: The Exhibit*. Reggio Emilia: Reggio Children.

Manning, J. (1956) *Dickens on Education*. Toronto: University of Toronto Press.

Manning, K. and Sharp, A. (1977) *Structuring Play in the Early Years at School*. London: Ward Lock Educational.

Manning-Morton, J. and Thorp, M. (2004) *Key Times for Play*. Buckingham: Open University Press.

Marsh, J. (ed.) (2005a) *Popular Culture, New Media and Digital Literacy in Early Childhood*. London: RoutledgeFalmer.

Marsh, J. (2005b) 'Digikids: young children, popular culture and media', in N. Yelland (ed.), *Critical Issues in Early Childhood Education*. Buckingham: Open University Press.

Marsh, J. and Thompson, P. (2001) 'Parental involvement in literacy development using media texts', *Journal of Research in Reading* 24(3), 266–78.

Martinez, L. (1998) 'Gender equity policies and early childhood education', in N. Yelland (ed.), *Gender in Early Childhood*. London: Routledge, pp. 115–30.

Mason, C. (1886) *The Home Schooling Series: Volume 1: Home Education. The education and training of children under nine*. Oxford: The Scrivener Press.

Mason, C. (1896) *The Home Schooling Series: Volume 2: Parents and Children. A practical study of educational principles*. Oxford: The Scrivener Press.

Mason, C. (1904) *The Home Schooling Series: Volume 3: Home and School Education. The training of education of children over nine*. Oxford: The Scrivener Press.

Mason, C. (1904) *The Home Schooling Series: Volume 4: Ourselves, Our Souls and Bodies. Book 1: Self knowledge. Book 2: Self direction*. Oxford: The Scrivener Press.

Mason, C. (1905) *The Home Schooling Series: Volume 5: Some Studies in the formation of character*. Oxford: The Scrivener Press.

Mason, C. (1923) *An Essay Towards a Philosophy of Education*. Oxford: The Scrivener Press.

Mason, C. (1955) *The Home Schooling Series*. Oxford: The Scrivener Press.

Meadows, S. and Cashdan, A. (1988) *Helping Children Learn: Contributions to a Cognitive Curriculum*. London: David Fulton Publishers.

Meek, M. (1982) *Learning to Read*. London: The Bodley Head.

Menegoi-Buzzi, I. (1999) 'A critical view of inclusion in Italy', in M. Chaltin, I. Menegoi-Buzzi, S. Phillips and N. Sylvestre (eds), *Integrating Children with Special Educational Needs (Handicapped) in Ordinary Schools: Case Studies in Europe*. Milan: IRRSAE, Lombardia.

Merleau-Ponty, M. (1962) *Phenomenology of Perception*. London: Routledge.

Miller, B. (1941) *George Muller: Man of Faith and Miracles*. Minneapolis, MN: Bethany House.

Miller, P. (1983) *Theories of Developmental Psychology*. San Francisco, CA: W. H. Freeman and Company.

Mills, R. W. and Mills, R. M. (1998) 'Child of our time: variations in adult views of childhood with age', *International Journal of Early Years Education* 6(1), 75–85.

Murphy, C. (1991) *Emil Molt and the Beginnings of the Waldorf School Movement*. Edinburgh: Floris Books.

Molt, E. (1919) *Emil Molt and the beginnings of the Waldorf School movement: Sketches from an autobiography*. Edinburgh: Floris Books, 1991.

Montessori, M. (1914) *Dr Montessori's Own Handbook*. New York: Schocken Books.

Montessori, M. (1962) *Education for a New World*. Wheaton, II: Theosophical Press.

Montessori, M. (1963) *The Secret of Childhood*. Calcutta: Orient Longmans.

Montessori, M. (1964) *The Absorbent Mind*. Wheaton, II: Theosophical Press.

Montessori, M. (1964) *The Montessori Method*. New York: Schocken Books.

Moss, P. (1989) *The United Nations Conventions on the Rights of the Child: Articles and Summary Commentary*. UNESCO/NCB.

Moyles, J. (ed.) (1994) *The Excellence of Play*. Buckingham: Open University Press.

Murphy, D. J. (1995) *Comenius: A Critical Reassessment of his Life and Work*. Dublin: Irish Academic Press.

Murray, P. and Penman, J. (1996) *Let Our Children Be*. Sheffield: Parents with Attitude.

Myers, R. (1993) *Attention by International Organisations to Early Childhood Care and Development: An Analysis of United Nations World Reports, 1993*. Early Childhood Care and Development website: http://www.ecdgroup.com

NACCCE (National Advisory Committee on Creative and Cultural Education) (1999) *All Our Futures: Creativity, Culture and Education*. London: Department for Children, Schools and Families.

National Education League (1869) *Report of the First General Meeting of the Members of the National Education League*. Birmingham: National Education League.

Neill, A. S. (1916) *A Dominie's Log*. London: Herbert Jenkins.

Neill, A. S. (1939) *The Last Man Alive*. London: Gollancz.

Neill, A. S. (1960) *Summerhill: A Radical Approach to Child Rearing*. New York: Hart Publishing.

Neill, A. S. (1973) *Neill, Neill, Orange Peel!* New York: Hart Publishing.

Newman, F. and Holzman, L. (1993) *Lev Vygotsky: Revolutionary Scientist*. London: Routledge.

Ney, M. (1999) *Charlotte Mason*. Nottingham: Education Heretics Press.

Nutbrown, C. (1996) *Respectful Educators – Capable Learners: Children's Rights and Early Education*. London: Paul Chapman Publishing.

Nutbrown, C. (1998) 'Managing to include? Rights, responsibilities and respect', in P. Clough (ed.), *Managing Inclusive Education: From Policy to Experience*. London: Paul Chapman Publishing.

Nutbrown, C. (2006) *Threads of Thinking: Young Children Learning and the Role of Early Education* (3rd edn). London: Sage.

Nutbrown, C. and Clough, P. (2004) 'Inclusion in the early years: conversations with European educators', *European Journal of Special Needs Education* 19(3), 311–39.

Nutbrown, C. and Hannon, P. (eds) (1997) *Preparing for Early Literacy Education with Parents: A Professional Development Manual*. Sheffield/Nottingham: NES Arnold/University of Sheffield, School of Education.

Nutbrown, C. and Hannon, P. (2003) 'Children's perspectives on early literacy: issues and methodologies', *Journal of Early Childhood Literacy* 3(2), 115–45.

Nutbrown, C., Hannon, P. and Collier, S. (1996) *Early Literacy Education with Parents: A Framework for Practice* (Video). Sheffield: The REAL Project/University of Sheffield, Sheffield University Television.

Nutbrown, C., Hannon, P. and Morgan, A. (2005) *Early Literacy Work with Families: Policy, Practice and Research*. London: Sage.

Oldfield, L. (2001) *Free to Learn: Introducing Steiner-Waldorf Early Childhood Education*. Stroud: Hawthorn Press.

Owen, R. (1836–44) *Book of the New Moral World*, 7 Parts. London (published as one volume, New York: G. Vale, 1845).

Owen, R. (1920) *The Life of Robert Owen: Written by Himself*. London: G. Bell and Sons.

Owen, R. (1927) *A New View of Society and Other Writings* [1812], ed. G. D. H. Cole. London: Dent.

Parker, C. (2002) 'Working with families on curriculum: developing shared understandings of children's mark making', in C. Nutbrown (ed.), *Research Studies in Early Childhood Education*. Stoke-on-Trent: Trentham Books.

Parker, D. (2005) *John Newsom: A Hertfordshire Educationist*. Hertfordshire: University of Hertfordshire Press.

Payton, S. (1984) *Developing Awareness of Print: A Child's First Steps Towards Literacy*. Birmingham: Educational Review Occasional Papers No. 2, University of Birmingham.

Penner, T. (1992) 'Socrates and the early dialogues', in R. Kraut (ed.), *The Cambridge Companion to Plato*. Cambridge: Cambridge University Press.

Pereera, S. (2000) 'Living with special educational needs: mothers' perspectives', in P. Clough and C. Nutbrown (eds) *Voices of Arabia: Essays in Educational Research*. Sheffield: University of Sheffield, School of Education.

Pestalozzi, J. H. (1907) *How Gertrude Teaches her Children: An Attempt to Help Mothers to Teach Their Own Children*. Trans. L. E. Holland and F. C. Turner (4th edn). London: Swan, Sonnenshein and Co.

Phillips, S. (2001) 'Special needs or special rights?', in L. Abbott and C. Nutbrown (eds), *Experiencing Reggio Emilia: Implications for Preschool Provision*. Buckingham: Open University Press.

Piaget, J. (1952) 'Jean Piaget (Autobiography)', in E. G. Boring (ed.), *A History of Psychology in Autobiography, Vol. 4*. Worcester MA: Clark University Press, pp. 237–56.

Piaget, J. (1929) *The Child's Conception of the World*. Harcourt, Brace: New York.

Piaget, J. and Inhelder, B. (1969) *The Psychology of the Child* [1966]. New York: Basic Books.

QCA (Qualifications and Curriculum Authority)/DfEE (Department for Education and Employment) (2000) *Curriculum Guidance for the Foundation Stage*. London: QCA/DfEE.

Rahilly, S. and Johnston, E. (2002) 'Opportunity for Childcare: The Impact of Government Initiatives in England upon Childcare Provision' *Social Policy & Administration* 36(5) 482–95.

Randell, S., Payne-Cook, E. and Marlow, P. (2004) *Ready for School – The Nursery Project: A Joint Initiative between Willowbrook School, Sure Start Exeter and Whipton First School*. National Evaluation of Sure Start: http://www.surestart.gov

Reggio Children (1995) *Le Fantane: Da un progetto per la construczione di u Luna Park degli uccellini [The Fountains: From a project for the construction of an amusement park for birds]*. Reggio Emilia: Reggio Children.

Richardson, M. (1935) *Writing and Writing Patterns*. London: University of London Press.

Roazen, P. (1976) *Erik H. Erikson: The Power and Limits of a Vision*. New York: The Free Press.

Roberts, S. and Howard, S. (2005) 'Watching Teletubbies: television and its very young audience', in J. Marsh (ed.), *Popular Culture, New Media and Digital Literacy in Early Childhood*. London: RoutledgeFalmer.

Rodman, F. R. (2003) *Winnicott: Life and Work*. Cambridge, MA: Perseus Publishing.

Roffey, S. (2001) *Special Needs in the Early Years: Collaboration, Communication and Co-ordination*. London: David Fulton Publishers.

Rogers, C. with Freiberg, H. J. (1993) *Freedom to Learn* (3rd edn). New York: Merrill.

Rogers, C. R. (1961) *On Becoming a Person: A Therapist's View of Psychotherapy*. Boston, MA: Houghton Mifflin.

Rogers, C. R. (1980) *A Way of Being*. Boston, MA: Houghton Mifflin.

Roscoe, B. (1990) 'Robin Tanner and the Crafts Study Centre', in B. Roscoe (ed.), *Tributes to Robin Tanner 1904–1988*. Bath: Holburne Museum and Crafts Study Centre.

Ross, D. D. and Brondy, E. (1987) 'Communicating with parents about beginning reading instruction', *Childhood Education* 63(4), 270–4.

Rousseau, J. J. (1979) *Emile, or On Education* [1762]. Trans. A. Bloom. New York: Basic Books.

Rousseau, J. J. (1993) *The Social Contract and Discourses* [1762/1750]. Trans. G. D. H. Cole. London: Everyman.

Rouse Selleck, D., Goldschmeid, E., and Elfer, P (2003) *Key Persons in the Nursery: Building Relationships for Quality Provision London*: David Fulton.

Rusk, R. R. (1954) *The Doctrines of the Great Educators* (2nd edn). London: Macmillan.

Santas, G. X. (1979) *Socrates: Philosophy in Plato's Early Dialogues*. London: Routledge and Kegan Paul.

Santrock, J. (1996) *Child Development*. Dubuque, IA: Brown and Benchmark Publishers.

Schaeffer Macauley, S. (1984) *For the Children's Sake: Foundations of Education for Home and School*. Westchester, IL: Crossway.

Schickedanz, J. (1990) *Adam's Righting Revolutions*. Portsmouth, NH: Heinemann.

Schupack, H. and Wilson, B. (1997) *The "R" Book: Reading, Writing and Spelling: The Multisensory Structured Language Approach*. Baltimore, MD: The International Dyslexia Association.

Schiller, C. (1951) 'How come change?' in C. Griffin-Beale (ed.) *Christian Schiller in this own Words* (1979) London: A. & C Black.

Schiller, C. (1979) *Christian Schiller in His Own Words*, ed. C. Griffin-Beale. London: A. & C. Black.

Schweinhart, L. J., Barnes, H. V. and Weikart, D. P. (1993) *Significant Benefits: The High Scope Perry Preschool Study through age 27*. Monograph of the High Scope Educational Research Foundation, 10. Ypsilanti, MI: High Scope Press.

Schweinhart, L. J., Montie, J., Xiang, Z., Barnett, W. S., Belfield, C. R., & Nores, M. (2005). *Lifetime effects: The High/Scope Perry Preschool study through age 40*. (Monographs of the High/Scope Educational Research Foundation, 14). Ypsilanti, MI: High/Scope Press.

Sharp, A. (2003) *Sure Start Ravensdale Breastfeeding Survey*, November 2003. National Evaluation of Sure Start: www.surestart.gov

Sharp, C. (1995) *School Entry and the Impact of Season of Birth on Attainment*, Research Summary (September). Slough: National Foundation for Educational Research in England and Wales.

Sheffield LEA (1986) *Nursery Education: Guidelines for Curriculum, Organisation and Assessment*. Sheffield: City of Sheffield Education Department.

Sheldon, D. and Blythe, G. (1993) *The Whales' Song*. London: Red Fox.

Silber, K. (1960) *Pestalozzi: The Man and his Work*. London: Routledge and Kegan Paul.

Siraj-Blatchford, I. (1994) *The Early Years: Laying the Foundations for Racial Equality*. Stoke-on-Trent: Trentham Books.

Skinner, B. F. (1938) *The Behavior of Organisms: An Experimental Analysis*. New York: Alfred A. Knopf.

Skinner, B. F. (1953) *Science and Human Behavior*. New York: Macmillan.

Skinner, B. F. (1972) *Beyond Freedom and Dignity*. New York: Alfred A. Knopf.

Skinner, B. F. (1974) *About Behaviorism*. New York: Alfred A. Knopf.

Skinner, B. F. (1976) *Particulars of My Life*. New York: Alfred A. Knopf.

Skinner, B. F. (1976) *Walden Two*. New York: Macmillan.

Smith, F. (1976) 'Learning to read by reading', *Language Arts* 53 (March), 297–9, 322.

Smith, L. (1996) *Critical Readings on Piaget*. London: Routledge.

Spinka, M. (1967) *John Amos Comenius: That Incomporable Moravian* (2nd edn). New York: Russell and Russell.

Steiner, R. (1947) *The Study of Man*. London: Anthroposophic Press.

Steiner, R. (1980) *Rudolf Steiner: An Autobiography*. Blauvelt, NY: Steinerbooks.

Steiner, R. (1995) *The Kingdom of Childhood: Introductory Talks on Waldorf Education*. Seven lectures and answers to questions given in Torquay, 12–20 August 1924. Translated by Rudolf Steiner Press. Hudson, NY: Anthroposophic Press.

Steiner, R. (1996a) *The Education of the Child: And Early Lectures on Education* [1924]. Hudson, NY: Anthroposophic Press.

Steiner, R. (1996b) *The Foundations of Human Experience*, Hudson, NY: Anthroposophic Press (originally published as *The Study of Man*, 1947).

Sure Start (2003) The New Sure Start Leaflet. Ref: SUULeaflet 01/12/03. Available online at: http://www.surestart.gov.uk/_doc/P0000783.pdf

Sure Start (2005) 'Inspring creativity', available online at: http://www.surestart.gov.uk/resources/childcareworkers/inspringcreativity

Sutton-Smith, B. (1997) *The Ambiguity of Play*. Cambridge, MA: Harvard University Press.

Sylva, K. (1994) 'The impact of early learning on children's later development', Appendix C in C. Ball, *Start Right: The Importance of Early Learning*. London: Royal Society for the Arts, pp. 84–96.

Sylva, K., Roy, C. and Painter, M. (1980) *Child Watching at Playgroup and Nursery*. London: Grant McIntyre.

Szretzer, R. (1964) "The origins of full-time compulsory education at five", *British Journal of Educational Studies*, Vol. XIII, No. 1, pp. 16–28.

Tanner, L. N. (1997) *Dewey's Laboratory School: Lessons for Today*. New York: Teachers College Press.

Tanner, R. (1977) 'The way we have come'. Lecture to the Plowden Conference, date. London: Bishop Grosseteste College.

Taylor, J. (2001) *Handwriting: A Teacher's Guide – Multisensory Approaches to Assessing and Improving Handwriting Skills*. London: David Fulton Publishers.

Thorne, B. (1992) *Carl Rogers*. London: Sage.

Tizard, B., Phelps, J. and Plewis, I. (1975) 'Play in preschool centres: play measures and their relation to age, sex and IQ', *Journal of Child Psychology and Psychiatry* 17, 251–62.

Tobin, J. J., Wu, D. Y. H. and Davidson, D. H. (1989) *Preschool in Three Cultures: Japan, China and the United States*. London: Yale University Press, pp. 2–11.

Visser, J., Cole, T. and Daniels, H. (2003) 'Inclusion for the difficult to include', in M. Nind, K. Sheehy and K. Simmons (eds), *Inclusive Education: Learners and Learning Contexts*. London: David Fulton Publishers.

Vygotsky, L. S. (1980) *Mind in Society: The Development of Higher Psychological Processes*. Cambridge, MA: Harvard University Press.

Vygotsky, L. S. (1986) *Thought and Language*. Boston, MA: MIT Press.

Wall, K. (2003) *Special Needs and Early Years: A Practitioners' Guide*. London: Paul Chapman Publishing.

Wallace, E. R. (1983) *Freud and Anthropology: A History and Reappraisal*. New York: International Universities Press.

Walmsley, J. (1969) *Neill and Summerhill: A Pictorial Study*. Baltimore, MD: Penguin.

Wedge, P. and Prosser, H. (1973) *Born to Fail?* London: Arrow Books, in association with the National Children's Bureau.

Weinberger, J. (1996) *Literacy Goes to School – The Parents' Role in Young Children's Literacy Learning*. London: Paul Chapman Publishing.

Weinberger, J., Pickstone, C. and Hannon, P. (eds) (2005) *Learning from Sure Start: Working with Young Children and their Families*. Buckingham: Open University Press.

Welchman, K. (2000) *Erik Erikson: His Life, Work, and Significance*. Philadelphia, PA: Open University Press.

Wells, G. (1987) *The Meaning Makers: Children Learning Language and Using Language to Learn*. London: Hodder and Stoughton.

Whalley, M. and the Pen Green Centre Team (2007) *Involving Parents in their Children's Learning* (2nd edn). London: Paul Chapman Publishing.

Whitehurst, G. J., Epstein, J. N., Angell, A. L., Payne, D. A., Crone, D. A. and Fischel, J. E. (1994) 'Outcomes of an emergent literacy intervention in Head Start', *Journal of Educational Psychology* 86(4), 542–55.

Williams, M. (1922) *The Velveteen Rabbit: Or How Toys Become Real*. New York: Avon Books.

Winnicott, D. W. (1947) *Hate in the Transference*. New York. Aron Books.

Winnicott, D. W. (1953) 'Transitional objects and transitional phenomena', *International Journal of Psychoanalysis* 34, 89–97.

Winnicott, D. W. (1957) *Mother and Child: A Primer of First Relationships*. New York: Basic Books.

Winnicott, D. W. (1964) *The Child, the Family and the Outside World*. Harmondsworth: Penguin.

Winnicott, D. W. (1965) *The Family and Individual Development*. London: Tavistock Publications.

Winnicott, D. W. (1971) *Playing and Reality*. London: Tavistock Publications.

Winnicott, D. W. (1984) *Deprivation and Delinquency*. London: Tavistock Publications.

Winnicott, D. W. (1988) *Human Nature*. London: Free Association Books.

Winnicott, D. W. (1993) *Talking to Parents*. Workingham and Cambridge, MA: Addison-Wesley.

Winnicott, D. W. (1996) *Thinking about Children*. London: Karnac Books.

Wise, L. and Glass, C. (2000) *Working with Hannah: A Special Girl in a Mainstream School*. London: RoutledgeFalmer.

Wokler, R. (1995) *Rousseau*. Oxford: Oxford University Press.

Wollheim, R. (1971) *Freud*. London: Fontana.

Wood, D., McMahon, L. and Cranstoun, Y. (1980) *Working with Under Fives*. London: Grant McIntyre.

Wood, L. and Bennett, N. (1997) 'The rhetoric and reality of play: teachers' thinking and classroom practice', *Early Years* 17(2), 22–7.

Wordsworth, W. (1888) *The Complete Poetical Works*, with an introduction by John Morley. London: Macmillan and Co.

Yelland, N. and Grieshaber, S. (1998) 'Blurring the edges', in N. Yelland (ed.), *Gender in Early Childhood*. London: Routledge, pp. 1–11.

Some historical archives and other sources consulted

B. F. Skinner Foundation
http://www.bfskinner.org

Comenius Museum
http://www.mjakub.cz/english/index.php?idm=37

Early Childhood Care and Development website
http://www.ecdgroup.com

Florence Nightingale Letters at the Clendening Library
http://clendening.kumc.edu/dc/fn/flochron.html

Institute of Education of the University of London Archives
http://www.ioe.ac.uk/library/archives

J. A. Comenius and the Czech School
http://www.pmjak.cz/English/indexen.htm

Lev Vygotsky Archive
http://www.marxists.org/archive/vygotsky

National Arts Education Archive (Trust)
http://www.24hourmuseum.org.uk

Steiner-Waldorf Fellowship
http://www.steinerwaldorf.org.uk/teaching

The British and Foreign School Society Archives
http://www.bfss.org.uk/archive

The Rousseau Association
http://www.rousseauassociation.org

The University of Sheffield Library Special Collections and Archives: Education Historical Collection
http://www.shef.ac.uk/library/special/educhist.pdf

The National Society for Religious Education
http://www.natsoc.org.uk/society/history

Author Index

Subject Index